CW01262567

CHIMES FROM
A WOODEN BELL

CHIMES FROM A WOODEN BELL

A hundred years in the life of a Euro-Armenian family

TAQUI ALTOUNYAN

I.B. TAURIS & CO. LTD
Publishers
London · New York

Published in 1990 by
I.B. Tauris & Co Ltd
110 Gloucester Avenue
London NW1 8JA

175 Fifth Avenue
New York
NY 10010

In the United States of America, and Canada
distributed by
St Martin's Press
175 Fifth Avenue
New York
NY 10010

Copyright 1990 by Taqui Altounyan

All rights reserved. Except for brief quotations in a review, this book, or any part thereof, must not be reproduced in any form without permission in writing from the publisher.

British Library Cataloguing in Publication Data
Altounyan, Taqui
    Chimes from a wooden bell.
    1. Great Britain.   Social life, 1850s–1950s
    I. Title
941.0823

ISBN 1-85043-239-2

Typeset in Baskerville 10½ on 12 pt. by
Columns Design & Production Services Ltd
Printed and Bound in Great Britain by
Redwood Press Limited, Melksham, Wiltshire

To
MARIANNE ELIZABETH ARAXI SHEPHERD
born 1987
and to the memory of
ROGER EDWARD COLLINGWOOD ALTOUNYAN
1922–1988

Acknowledgements

I wish to thank: Odile and Albert Hourani for their constant encouragement and sympathy, Christopher Walker for his book *Armenia, The Survival of a Nation*, Vera Collingwood for coming with me to Aghtamar and handing me those five almonds, Sirvart, Susan and Levon Chilingirian for welcoming me back so enthusiastically from those travels, also Mary Pyves, Penny Robbins, Philip Dalziel, Roger Wardale.

All these and a few more I thank for listening over the years to my endless talk about family – and still remaining friends.

In Ottoman times Armenian churches were not allowed to have metal bells. Instead, they used the *simandrum*, a thick wooden board suspended by two chains to a beam in the church porch for the priest to hit with a stick. The cathedral in Jerusalem still has one. This cracking sound of wood on wood is a harsh reminder of the *charcharank*, or torture, endured by so many generations of Armenians. Other reminders are words like *char* (bad), *chaghil* (reprimand), *chaghchagh* (a hammer), *chaghchaghil* (to break in pieces, overwhelm), and *chartell* (to massacre).

PART I

The unknown remembered gate

We shall not cease from exploration
And the end of our exploring
Will be to arrive where we started
And to know the place for the first time
Through the unknown remembered gate
When the last of earth left to discover
Is that which it was at the beginning.

T.S. Eliot, 'Little Gidding – 1942',
Four Quartets

Aleppo is a town of eminent consequence and in all ages its fame has flown high. The kings who have sought its hand in marriage are many and its place in our souls is dear. How many battles has it provoked and how many white blades have been drawn against it? ... the town is as old as eternity yet new, although it has never ceased to be. Its days and years have been long ... Oh city of wonder! It stays, but its kings depart.

The Travels of Ibn Jubayr, 1182
Ibn Jubayr (1145–1217)

Introduction

My grandfather, Aram Assadour Altounyan, was pure Armenian, born in the original homeland, the Caucasus mountains, Ararat and the Anatolian plateau, today eastern Turkey. The Armenians, as an ethnic group, were part of a migration of Indo–European tribes which, in the first millenium BC, came from the East into Europe. Splitting off early from the other tribes, the Armenians remained in the Anatolian plateau where they met and mingled with the Urartians and evolved their own language. The first king of the Urartians was called Aram, like my grandfather, but they were not of the same people. The fact that the people who are known to the rest of the world as 'Armenians' call themselves 'Haïk' suggests the merging of two tribes after the fall of Urartu. The extreme wildness of the terrain they inhabited dictated the formation of kingdoms or baronacies, individualistic and tough but so small that their only hope of survival lay in alliances with each other or with other, larger powers; this has been the pattern throughout Armenian history. Many of the Anatolian mountains run east and west, forming a corridor for invading armies, and the Armenian kingdoms were often desirable buffer states between great powers.

In AD 301 the Armenians adopted Christianity as their state religion. This was important because it inclined them permanently towards the West. In AD 404 the invention of the Armenian alphabet and the translation of the Bible into the vernacular further defined them as a nation. A strong Arab invasion in the ninth century and the establishment of a hegemony lasting two hundred years created a peaceful period in which Armenian culture reached its highest peak. This was the golden age of the kingdom of Ani and many of the cathedrals, the battered remains of which still stand today, date from this time. Stone-carving and metalwork were distinctive national skills. The Mongol invasions of the eleventh and thirteenth centuries put an end to this. Thousands of Armenians fled south to the protection of the last emperor of Byzantium who, in 1198, enabled them to establish the new kingdom of Cilicia round the town of Antioch in the north-east corner of the Mediterranean. After the fall of Cilicia in 1375, Armenians lingered on in the region round Aleppo and eventually became subjects of the Ottoman Empire (1453-1920).

In this empire, which in its time was equal with China and the Holy Roman Empire, the Armenians played an important part as bankers, merchants and administrators, as well as skilled craftsmen, and felt that their fate was linked with that of their host country. This false sense of security was heightened by the Turkish 'millet' system which gave Jews and Christians freedom to worship as they wished provided their religious leaders were loyal to the sultan.

By the end of the nineteenth century, however, the Ottoman Empire had begun to weaken and Russia and the emerging European powers eagerly competed for its fragmented territories. Hoping to arrest the decline, in 1896 a group calling themselves the Young Turks formed the Committee of Union and Progress. At first, both Turks and Armenians in the Ottoman capital of Istanbul could hardly help working together, influenced as they were by the revolutionary spirit sweeping Europe. The intellectuals pinned their hopes on the Young Turks, who got rid of the last and most corrupt sultan, Abdel Hamid; the Armenians had already begun to form their own political parties. But it became all too easy to blame the Christian minority – the Armenians – for everything which went wrong, and when, in 1914, Turkey came into the war on the side of Germany against Russia, the Armenians were suspected of sympathizing with the enemy. Armenian soldiers in the Turkish Army were disarmed and shot and their families deported. Whole villages were emptied of their Armenian populations, the women, children and old people being driven into the desert where they had little hope of survival. Between 1915 and 1923 about one-third of the Armenians in Turkey were killed in this way.

Today, only one-tenth of the historic homeland, namely the Armenian Soviet Socialist Republic, has any sizeable Armenian population. All of eastern Turkey, where my grandfather was born in Sivas, remains barren and largely underpopulated. The survivors and their progeny are scattered all over the world.

When the frontiers of Soviet Armenia and Soviet Azerbaijan were being decided after World War One, Armenia was allocated the worst land. Neighbouring Azerbaijan, with its Islamic population and its invaluable oilfields, acquired districts where many Armenians lived. With the advent of Gorbachov the Armenians felt encouraged to voice their long-held grievance about this, and in the last few years the sense of grievance has grown, fuelled by the earthquake of 1987 which some believe was caused by the government nuclear programme. Certainly, the rebuilding has not been helped by frontier troubles. More and more Armenians are leaving the country and visitors report a sullen mood of depression. But adversity has always brought amazing resilience; the Armenians are, after all, professional survivors with centuries of practice behind them.

My grandfather left his birthplace in central Anatolia as soon as he could. After his father's death in about 1860, when he was seven, his best hope of escape was to train as a doctor, which he did with the help of American missionaries, first in their mission hospitals in Turkey, and subsequently in America and Europe. Back in Turkey, and fully qualified, he married the Irish–Scottish matron of a mission hospital, and the couple set out on their own, touring the towns and villages of the south as a mobile medical team. This undoubtedly saved my grandfather's life because, by the time the most serious massacres of Armenians began, he was well established in Aleppo which, although still at that time part of the Ottoman Empire, was an Arab town. Also, by then, he had acquired an impressive reputation as a doctor, and the Turks considered him too valuable to destroy.

My grandfather was sixty by the time he got permission from the Turks to build a hospital. He devoted the next thirty years of his long life to making it into a sort of super 'space hospital' or 'Mayo Clinic' hung between East and West and as good as any in the world. He dared to hope that future generations would be as single-minded as himself.

The colours of my grandfather's life stand out as bright as those of the beautiful carpets he loved to collect, but my father's pattern is more blurred and hard to follow. Ernest was born far from the Armenian homeland, in London, and brought up by his Irish mother as an English gentleman. His inherited toughness was needed to help him survive an English preparatory school, and he used a lot of energy trying to forget he was Armenian, imagining himself as a poet as well as a doctor.

While at Rugby, his life was transformed by meeting Robin Collingwood who invited him home to Lanehead where he competed with Arthur Ransome for a place in that idealized family. With Armenian persistence my father persuaded one of the Collingwood daughters to marry him and so managed to transplant some of the Collingwood atmosphere to Aleppo. His wife, Dora, was fascinated by her new country where she raised and educated five children and painted many pictures of the Syrian landscape. Although he spent most of his life in Aleppo, Ernest could count among his friends members of the Bloomsbury group, as well as T.E. Lawrence.

My brother Roger, born in Aleppo in 1922, was, in his turn, temperamentally more like his grandfather, having inherited the old man's sense of being at ease with the world. He tried to work in Aleppo with his father for a time and he found it hard, but, in the end, it was the xenophobia of a young, developing Syria which forced him to leave. He then made a new career for himself by inventing a drug for the treatment of asthma.

As for myself, I was the eldest of Dora's and Ernest's five children, and was born in Hampstead in 1917, where my next sister followed in 1919. Two more sisters were born in Aleppo in 1920 and 1926. When my grandfather and parents were dead and I was grown up, I found the courage to return to Aleppo and to travel in lands previously forbidden. And I began to discover the truth behind the whispers and hints of my childhood, and to learn for myself the fate of the Armenian people.

Chapter One

My Armenian grandfather was born in 1854, the first year of the Crimean War. The present House of Commons was built in that year and Big Ben was cast. With his usual astuteness he managed to be in time for the Industrial Revolution and the American missionaries who were beginning to take education into Turkey. Robert College in Istanbul was founded in 1860 and the American College in Aintab in eastern Turkey at about the same time. Grandfather was among the first of the bright boys to be sent to be educated in the United States; somehow he managed to be a step ahead all his life. 'Mischievous as a young mule' or 'an amazing old man', Aram Assadour Altounyan always knew exactly what he wanted out of life.

We called him 'Black Grandpa' because of his hair, to distinguish him from our 'White Grandpa' in England. He left Sivas when he was fifteen and never went back. He pronounced it 'Swazz' with a soft look in his eyes, a tragic look which was usually not noticed because of the whole perky optimism of his bearing, but which was a permanent memory of what had happened to him and his family all those years ago. I remember him laughing, his eyes seemed to glow and the curvy, joyous lines made his mouth the most important feature in his face – except for his extraordinary nose. Difficult to describe, this nose: not hawklike, more human than that, dominant and awe-inspiring yet somehow delicate – the nose of an Arab sheikh perhaps, yet with that peculiar Armenian shape. It was not handed down either to my father or my brother. It was unique. His black beard and curly black hair, the proud way he carried his small but upright figure, his quick, sure movements, all enhanced and set off this important nose. And his careful way of dressing – also not inherited by my father or brother – showed that he had not forgotten how hard he had worked to buy his first set of European clothes all those years ago as a medical apprentice.

My grandfather's odyssey had taken place, it seemed to us, in a land a million miles away, many thousands of years before we were born. Different rules from the ones we knew had shaped his life. Sivas was, in fact, only a few hundred miles away from our home in Aleppo – a good car would have taken us there in a day – but we could never go there because we were Armenian. We could only listen to his stories and wonder.

Although Black Grandpa spoke of Sivas as if it were a garden of Eden, European travellers disagreed. According to H.F.B. Lynch, who travelled in Armenia in the nineteenth century, the old Roman town of Sebastea, situated in the north of the great central plateau of Anatolia, was in a landscape 'bare as the scalp of death and scarcely decently clad with vegetation'. The terror and inhumanity of the scene was enhanced by extinct volcanoes and landlocked lakes, their waters a milky soda blue, which rose and fell mysteriously though they had no outlet. Not a single tree grew naturally, the only streak of green being gardens round human habitation. The village houses were hardly more than mean heaps of stones roughly pulled together, quite dwarfed by the huge cones of hay and dung-cakes stacked around them, ready for the winter. When the snow came the little houses were almost buried and the dung and fodder had to be dug out. Neighbours were recognized by their footsteps over the roofs because the streets were impassable.

Sebastea was capital of the Roman province of Capadocia on the trade route from the Far East to Constantinople. Although, by the time Black Grandpa was born, there were other, quicker ways of getting to Constantinople, the velvety sound of camels' feet on sand along the highway must have been the background to his baby dreams just as they were to mine, much later, in Aleppo.

There were almost as many Armenians as Turks in Sivas in the middle of the nineteenth century and luckily the first missionaries from America were beginning to come there to establish their colleges and hospitals. They wrote encouragingly to their wives, 'Sivas has a healthful climate with lots of good water'. In all Christian honesty they had to add, 'The streets are unpaved, full of deep mud, and the sidewalks, when there are any, are of rough cobbles'. As they still are!

The Altounyan family were allowed to have red tiles on their big two-storey house near the main square. This shows that they were people of some standing. Black Grandpa's father and his two brothers were educated; they were also large and brawny which was useful. In those days before 1915, Turks and Armenians lived together in neighbourly friendliness though the little boys sometimes played a rough game of 'Turks and Armenians' in which no one wanted to be the Armenians. The worse incident, before things got really bad, was that the family's fierce watch-dog was found one morning in a side-alley with its throat cut.

Assadour, as Black Grandpa was called then, grew up in the two-storey house with its walled garden. In the summer the family lived in the open air. The lower part of the house was stables for the family horses, donkeys, cows, sheep and goats. It was Assadour's job to take the animals out to the common grazing ground. In the evening he had to watch very carefully to see how the lambs behaved with the sheep to know if he had the right ones. He learned all his lessons in human behaviour from animals, he used to say.

According to the legend, Assadour was only seven when his father became 'mortally ill'. His two uncles were apothecaries or chemists and, at that time, there was already an American missionary doctor in the town. The boy had been taught to read by his mother, who was more educated than most women because she was the daughter of a priest. The story has it that the little boy reached down a 'medical book' (was it in Armenian?) and began to spell out his father's symptoms. He read that in just ten days his father would either recover or die. Coolly he drew out a calendar and hung it on the wall – on the tenth day his father died. Assadour vowed he was going to be a doctor.

He was the eldest of the family and there was very little

money. He bullied his two brothers into getting what they could out of the 'useless school'. In their times off they wandered the hills round Sivas with their catapults, shooting small birds to roast over a fire and eat whole, bones and all. One day they thought they'd try to move a huge bolder on the side of the hill. They pushed and pushed and suddenly it began to roll down the hill, faster and faster towards the main road. 'We did not wait to see what would happen. We just ran away into the hills as fast as we could. When we crept back in the evening we were very relieved to find that no one had been killed.' The events of my grandfather's life were remembered haphazardly – not always the most important survived to be retold.

When the American missionary Dr West first came to Sivas and met my grandfather, he knew no Turkish or Armenian and Assadour knew no English, but there was a certain down-to-earth stubbornness about both their characters. Dr West boasted that he could 'feel the pulse, look at the tongue, thump the chest, cut out tumours, without any knowledge of the language – and so have the advantage over the preaching missionary'. He began in a small and cautious way, offering medicines, as well as tracts, to anyone who came to him for help. Very soon his fame spread north and south towards the Black Sea and the Mediterranean. Patients even came to him on donkeys from Erzurum two hundred miles away. 'The patients are stupid and gullible', wrote Dr West to the *Missionary Herald*. He came to despair of the way 'the Oriental expects his doctor to work miracles. If he is not cured he goes somewhere else. If a small dose is good, a large one would be more so. They have been known to eat mustard poultices. The servant is sometimes bullied into taking medicine for the master. And they never never carry out instructions as to diets.'

So the missionary doctor must have been more than pleased when the bright-looking boy presented himself at the surgery door. With his help, Assadour learned a little English or dog Latin, or whatever language is required to make up simple prescriptions, and he soon started a little amateur surgery on his own. 'I learned to open up the abscesses of my little friends, holding the sharp side of the blade upwards to avoid cutting into any deep vessel.' Gallstone extractions were exciting and lucrative: 'As soon as the stone appeared I would snatch it away and hide it to sell to the relative for a good baksheesh [tip].' There was always plenty of practical work and a lot could be learned by watching and assisting. Operations were done on a kitchen table or two packing cases put together. The anaesthetic was always chloroform until, one day, the patient died and Dr West and his assistants were badly beaten up. After this ether was the rule.

My grandfather was always sorry for Europeans and American missionaries – they seemed to him so vulnerable. So many of the foreign doctors and their families died of typhoid but 'the indigenous population are constantly taking in small doses of infection and so acquire a certain degree of immunity'. Dr West died of typhoid. With four of his children, he 'went to a better life'.

In between helping Dr West, Assadour gave a hand to his apothecary uncles. He earned his keep by helping in the house, sweeping, cooking and shopping. All his medical books were earned by doing odd jobs: it took 140 hours of trench-digging to earn him his Grey's *Anatomy*, first published just four years after he was born. After Dr West had gone, there was no one to teach him English, so he learned in the traditional way, looking up words in a dictionary in the evening, after his other work was done, by the light of an oil-lamp.

As there was a tradition of medicine in the family, there was usually plenty of opportunity to learn. For instance: 'Not much attention was given to antisepsis in those days – surgeons rarely washed their hands before operating – but *always after*.' But he learned about antiseptics from his cousin dealing with an accident! A boy had fallen on his side on a cherry tree branch so that part of it went right through his abdomen. When they at last dared to pull the branch out, a large lump of intestine came with it. 'My cousin took a basin and carefully washed the intestine in warm water to which he had added a few drops of carbolic acid. He then pushed back the gut and stitched the wound. The boy recovered.'

Assadour's big break came when his cousin married a Dr Siouni who had been among the first of the Armenian boys sent to America for training and who had now been appointed

Professor of Medicine at the new college at Aintab. In 1878 Assadour was asked to go with the bride, to be her husband's assistant. He was by then about twenty-four and eager to further his studies.

The country between Sivas and Aintab is made up of mountains running east and west, so the caravan had to keep crossing high passes. On one of these they were attacked by brigands and were left only with the clothes they stood up in. All was lost: the bridal trousseau; the wedding furniture; and, worst of all, the bright new surgical instruments from America.

The Central Turkey College Medical School turned out to be 'the funniest imaginable'. The Professor of Surgery had quarrelled with everyone and left. There was now only the Professor of Chemistry. There were no classrooms, no laboratories – only one room containing two chairs and a skeleton. The daily lecture was taken out of the only textbook the school possessed. Nothing daunted, my grandfather got through all the exams and tests there happened to be and became a tutor. He was pleasantly surprised that students from other departments attended his lectures because they were amusing. The anatomy classes were livened up by gravediggers coming in with bits of bone to sell. The great problem was to get bodies for dissection. 'Our only source was wintertime stealing from the graveyard. One day, one of the city cases died suddenly and we were anxious to make up a post-mortem to find out the cause of death,' my grandfather used to tell us in his funny, slightly stilted English. 'Having located the grave, we went out on a very stormy night and got the body.' Unfortunately they did not know that the burial was only temporary so the next day, when the real funeral was planned, the body was nowhere to be found. 'The whole town was in an uproar but medical students' habits were well known. They knew where to look but, kindly, allowed us to finish the post-mortem.' Grave-robbing was very common in those days, mostly for the valuable shrouds bodies were wrapped in. There is a comic story of a thief who barked like a dog while he worked 'so if any Armenian family living by the graveyard heard barking in the middle of the night, they would cross themselves knowing that Cousin Manouk was at his dirty work.'

Patients often insisted that the young tutor do their dressings because he was so gentle. From the baksheesh he got from this he bought his first suit of European clothes. It cost 15 Ottoman medgidis, twenty to the Turkish gold pound. Up to then he had been wearing the traditional peasant dress which Kurds in eastern Anatolia still wear: baggy trousers and a shirt, kept together at the waist by a huge shawl belt; over this an embroidered waistcoat and an ordinary tweed jacket. On his head he probably wore a red felt fez and, on his feet, shoes with turned-up toes. He would always take the shoes off when coming into a house and walk forward over the carpet wearing hand-knitted sheep's-wool socks.

The beautiful new European suit was acquired just in time for his journey to the United States in 1884. The American missionaries were looking for bright young men to send to America for training in medicine or preaching. Long researches through old issues of the *Missionary Herald* on scorching afternoons in Izmir brought out no more interesting details about my grandfather's journey than that 'seven boys [were] sent to Columbia University from Aintab College'. 'Native' orphaned boys did not have names in those days, however bright they might be. A mysterious letter among my files headed 'Pera Palace Hotel Constantinople', signed with a German name and dated 26 August (but no year), wishes Assadour 'the very best of luck on your coming attempt to swim the Bosporus'. Perhaps the meaning was symbolic.

In my grandfather's luggage were one or two bottles of liquid containing scabs of 'the Aleppo button sore', endemic in Aintab and Aleppo and elsewhere in the Ottoman Empire. He had been studying it for the past six years – on his own face! This was the subject of his doctoral thesis at Columbia, where he graduated over a hundred years ago now. The slightly stilted, meticulous style is familiar: 'The sore appearing singly or in numbers, on the exposed parts of the body, cicatrices slowly under a scab which resembles an oyster shell . . . Usually lasts a year and leaves a bad scar.' He could not say for certain but he thought it was caused by the bite or sting of some special insect particular to certain soils or climates. The favourite time for the sore to appear was the summer when most insects 'arrived at maturity'. 'It is not customary in these regions to sleep upon bedsteads. Most natives as a rule place their mattresses directly upon the ground in the yard or upon the roofs of the houses, on account of the troublesome heat in the buildings. Such a way of living seems favourable to the development of the button.' He observed that babies seldom got it, perhaps because their mothers kept them well swaddled. If the mother was careless and omitted the custom, taking the baby to her bed without the usual swaddling, 'it is most certain that in this latter case I have found the Aleppo button under the age of one year old'.

The learned professors of Columbia University, New York, solemnly listened to the young man from the Ottoman Empire defending his thesis. 'Contrary to the theories of French, German and British doctors,' he said in his slight Armenian accent, 'the sore is not caused by sandstorms, excessive heat, dirty habits, bad drinking water or a parasite burrowing under the skin.' Furthermore, it was not the famous old disease of lupus or any sort of venereal disease, 'and it is not confined to Aleppo,' declaimed the young doctor, 'but the name is that most frequently used by the profession for the boil found in Syria and Mesopotamia. It will be well to keep it until further research discloses the exact causation and pathology of the disease.'

The professors probably showed no surprise to learn that the only cure at that time was 'cod-liver oil taken internally and tincture of iodine externally'.

Having gained his doctorate in 1885, Dr A.A. Altounyan competed successfully for the post of house surgeon at a New York hospital: 'But my teacher, who knew my future ambitions, advised me not to stay but to go to Germany.' Because of this advice and the fact that he was expected back in Aintab sometime, he sold the position for a hundred dollars and turned eastwards again, taking as long as possible to get home.

In those days it was fairly easy for students to attend the laboratories of the famous for a few months or a year and to get a signed certificate of attendance. On his way back to Turkey and also on later visits to Germany, my grandfather attended the laboratories of such men as Koch, Bilroth, Czerni and Erb. The most important was Koch who had just succeeded in isolating the cholera bacillus. (My grandfather had to fight a constant battle against cholera in Aleppo. The first house he took there was chosen because it had a cellar whose temperature was just right for his cultures.) Even with his doctorate and a hundred dollars, Assadour was often very hungry. He remembered going into a restaurant and asking for their cheapest cheese. He did not expect it to be green and mouldy – he hadn't heard of gorgonzola. He learned German really well, paying for his lessons with flagons of beer. For the rest of his long life he felt more at home in Germany than in England or France, and he never let many years pass without going back there to be 'brushed up after the Aleppo dust'. Some of the stories he told us fifty years after were hard to believe. Stories of those times are like pebbles worn smooth with much handling. There must have been many incidents which never survived to be told. Unfortunately, his notebooks, written in beautiful copperplate with careful drawings, hardly yield a doodle or a personal note. There is, for instance, the story about the clinic – in Heidelberg was it? – where he found the students queuing up to look into a microscope. My grandfather asked the professor what they were examining. 'A new crystal,' he said. 'We are going to publish it next week.' When the uppish young man had had his squint he asked the professor what he had used for collecting the specimen in. 'An ordinary rubber cap,' was the reply. 'Then these crystals are possibly the granules of powder used to preserve the rubber,' my grandfather observed. All he got in answer then was a strange look. But when he went back a few days later, the professor shook hands very warmly and gave Assadour the chair next to his. At the end of every sentence of his lecture he turned to him to ask if it was correct.

Assadour's younger brother, Dikran, had remained in Aintab. When he heard about the doctorate, he borrowed a dictionary and wrote:

My dear Brother A.A. Altounyan MD at Heidelberg. My dear Brother I am very glad that full with errors nevertheless I have been happiness to write letter in English language. I may hope from God that successively filling my necessity in this language, he will deserve me one day that I have been learned perfectly this language. My beneficient brother I am very sorry that have been learned some English cannot write one good letter. Cannot write one common friendly letter without dictionary or to correct several times. All students of college are obliged to speak English language at the college but you cannot find one who can speak without errors. Your brother D.A. Altounyan. (Dated 16 March 1886)

The handwriting is good, but what did the elder brother think? These stumbling words, after the eloquence of the thesis, highlight the tremendous effort that must have been needed to progress. Dikran was not so much younger than Assadour.

Though he returned to Aintab in 1887 to work in a missionary hospital, as he had promised, the young doctor soon became restless. He could get on so much better on his own. He was fond of the American doctors but their Christian missionary principles were not his. For instance, when he went on an operating tour of the country, as he often did to make money, he never took on patients who were likely to die. In this way he built up a good reputation for himself. The American missionaries charitably took on everyone that came. Their reputations went down and down. We can only guess what the doctors at Aintab hospital thought when, in 1888, the newly returned young man went off into the blue, taking with him as his wife the matron Harriet Riddall who had just been expensively imported from Ireland. And it would be nice to know how she had been talked into linking her fate with the 'regrettable Armenian' who if not actually a heathen was probably near to it. Her family in Armagh were slightly relieved to hear that the Armenians had been the first nation to 'embrace Christianity': 'But an orphan, and without money, who had been sent by missionaries to pick up some sort of a degree in New York. A Turk might at least have been a gentleman, and rich, one of the ruling classes.'

I imagine a flurry of letters, written in violet ink, with spluttering pens and blots, from Armagh to that mission hospital in central Anatolia – invariably a month out of date. Harriet's three brothers were respectable Belfast businessmen.

'The Glen Riddell Genealogy' states that the family had been originally Lowland Scottish. It had split in 1745 when one part 'went out with' Prince Charles (Bonnie Prince Charlie), and the third son, Walter, left his family, went over to Ireland and was 'completely forgotten by them'. He even changed the spelling of his name. Harriet Riddall was his great-granddaughter. She must have had plenty of the Presbyterian qualities that made her ancestor leave Scotland. Once she decided a course of action was right there was no going back. She had already defied her three brothers when she decided to go out to Turkey 'to nurse the heathen'. It had been obvious to them that anything might happen.

The honeymoon cannot have been much different from the many operating tours the doctor had done when he was short of money. Only this time he had a wife riding side-saddle – much to the distress of the local horseowners who thought it damaged their animals. My grandfather rode in an American cowboy saddle, a present from one of his missionary friends. The local wooden ones were impossibly uncomfortable, with only dangerous twisted ropes for stirrups. The American saddle had stiff leather hoods for the feet. If a rider was thrown, his heel could never catch. And, at the end of a long ride, toecaps were not splattered with mud. The rest of the caravan consisted of mules carrying an astonishing assortment of glittering surgical instruments of German manufacture, and the precious glass tubes containing the Koch anticholera bacillus. At the very rear was the white-painted operating table, a shining advertisement for the young surgeon.

They travelled for weeks, going south all the time, from Diarbekir on the Tigris, its sinister black walls dominating the countryside, to Antioch on the Orontes, where Harriet was kept awake all night by creaking water-wheels. The rate of travel was about three miles per hour and they usually did twenty-five miles in a day. Before they finally settled in Aleppo, the couple made several such trips (indeed, their first daughter died while they travelled) to make enough money to go to England so that Assadour could take an intensive course in child medicine at St Mary's Hospital, Paddington – 'because I was ignorant of childish ailments'. My father, Ernest, was born in London in

The Unknown Remembered Gate

November 1889, and shortly afterwards Assadour and Harriet, together with their small son, arrived in Aleppo, looking for a home.

It was the unusual cleanness of the streets which first made them decide to settle in Aleppo. The whole town, built of white stone ageing to primrose or burnt orange, was frequently sluiced down with water because, the number of Jews, Christians and Muslims in the town being equal, weekend cleaning was at least three days long. Water ran in small rivulets down the stone steps onto the cobbled streets on Thursdays, Fridays and Saturdays.

Almost exactly 400 miles due south of Sivas, Aleppo lies in a shallow saucer of low rocky hills. The saucer is full of grey ashes and in the middle stands the castle like an inverted teacup. In the spring, for a very few weeks, the orange-coloured walls are like a golden crown on the green velvet cushion of the mound. Our travellers would have seen the minaret on the castle walls appear and disappear as they breasted each hill and, at last, the whole town laid out in its setting of gardens, the mosque domes bubbling up among flat rooftops with minarets like slim iris buds. The streets in the centre of the old town are still so narrow that in places it is possible to walk from one rooftop to another. In this upper world, animals graze on the lush plants that have sprung up between the stones, washing hangs out, children play precariously. On a terrace rooftop surrounded by flowers in pots, you can crane up at a minaret just above your head, put out a hand to feel the swell of the dome beside it, look down through a grating to watch life going on in the dark souk below.

Although Aleppo is on a crossroads, with important merchant routes running east and west, north and south, the castle in the centre is a constant reminder of very ancient history and gives the town a surprising stability. Damascus is tragically losing this as its fabulous gardens are built over. In Ernest's youth, 'the dour solid crabbed northern town left politics to Damascus, religion to Jerusalem, and the superficialities of European civilisation to Beirut'. It has not changed much today.

For over 4,000 years the town has grown, almost like a coral reef, all of a piece. Its position, commanding trade routes in every direction, meant continual nourishment, animation and stimulation. Not itself on the sea, it was only four days' ride from Alexandretta (known to the Elizabethans as Iskaneroon, and today called Iskenderun) where merchant ships constantly arrived. Carrier pigeons, with news of the ships' arrival, flew swiftly to the merchants waiting in Aleppo in their khans, the houses where they lived and did business. The Levant Company, formed by Queen Elizabeth at the end of the sixteenth century, had its headquarters in Constantinople. Shakespeare could be certain that his audiences knew the name, although he made a mistake about the geography, placing it on the coast.

The British merchants of the Levant Company had to compete with Italian, French and Dutch rivals and, of course, they had further to come. It was often younger sons who were sent out to try their luck in Aleppo and, sometimes, they stayed as long as thirty years. Some were even buried in the cemetery in Aleppo. Syria was then part of the Ottoman Empire and the Ottoman Turks often made life difficult for the merchants, imposing on them restrictions and curfews and making them wait many months for permission to trade. When, during the long summer months, cholera raged, they were isolated, by order, from the rest of the town, quarantined in their khans, and could only communicate over the rooftops, or by notes in cleft sticks poked through doors by servants. There was no street lighting, only lanterns, till long after the Altounyans, who had their own generator, settled there.

When the Altounyan caravan arrived in Aleppo, there was no shortage of doctors. All the foreign consulates had their own medical teams who were also allowed to practise in the town. There were also a great many government and military 'doctors'. However, according to my grandfather, the town had, up to his arrival, proved 'unlucky for surgeons'. He was the first doctor in Aleppo to charge money for a mere examination – even without a bottle of medicine. 'I am a merchant', he said in that town of merchants, 'all I have to sell is my time and my brains.'

He made his first clinic in 'The Street of the Butchers', taking care that it was on rising ground so that the open drains flowed away downhill. The old Arab house had two courtyards: in one he lived; in the other was 'what the people called my hospital'. It consisted, at that time, just of empty rooms and sixteen iron bedsteads which were, in themselves, unusual when almost everyone slept on the floor. Samovars provided all the hot water. The large oil-lamp which lit the operating room also heated the back of the surgeon's neck unbearably, so that night work was, if possible, avoided. Patients came from the town and from distant villages, bringing their own bedding. Relatives had to sleep beside the bed to do the nursing. There was not a single nurse in the whole town. Food was brought in from outside. Thermometers were unknown. The rich did not deign to stay in the so-called 'hospital': 'We had to operate in their houses, or send them home on stretchers'. And Assadour made his rich patients have their rooms specially scrubbed out and whitewashed before he would operate. Everything had to be paid for, immediately, in cash. Each night, before my grandfather would eat his supper, the day's earnings would be counted and transferred to three large cloth bags (one for silver, one for copper, one for gold) and these were put in the large dark wardrobe in his bedroom.

Always, there were plenty of jealous eyes watching the processions of doctor, stretchers, tables and equipment through the streets – looking, my grandfather said, like a 'Turkish wedding' – hoping fervently that the newcomer would crash. But well-managed miracles came to the rescue, as when he was called in to be one of the dozens of doctors attending on the daughter of Sultan Hamid's bodyguard, who had been exiled in Aleppo:

> I found four European and five military doctors who had been treating her for an acute case of tuberculosis. I went upstairs alone and examined the patient, and found that it was a serious case of typhoid. My colleagues wanted to 'eat me alive' when I gave my opinion. Thinking that I was in for trouble, they left me to it.

Two weeks later, the patient was recovering from typhoid. The girl came from a very good family. The Sultan was impressed.

Then there was the year of the specially bad cholera epidemic. The new doctor, with Western magic in his bag, had come at the right time. Sultan Hamid's fortune-teller had just predicted that his master would die of cholera coming from Aleppo. Twenty of the best Turkish doctors were already permanently stationed in Aleppo as an 'early warning', but 'the European' (or 'the American', as my grandfather was often called), with his culture plates and tubes, was the one who inspired confidence. Gradually he persuaded people to believe less in charms and amulets and more in simple hygiene such as: 'avoiding shaking hands or embracing each other so as not to spread infection; to carry in season a few sour grapes in the pocket to clean the mouth'. He did many real but simple cures by injecting large quantities of salt water. In this way he could resurrect many who appeared dead. The result of all this was that the Sultan issued an order that no one but 'the Armenian' (as he was also called) was to countersign any health report coming from Aleppo.

After five years in Aleppo and with no proper home yet, Assadour needed at least one more miracle before he could begin to build his dream hospital. 'Give us baksheesh and we will give you permission', he was still being told. He stubbornly refused. Again it was an exiled pasha who helped him. This one had developed cancer of the mouth. The Sultan would rather pay all expenses in Aleppo than have him come home. Miraculously, the patient was cured and, as a result, the permit to build a hospital was granted: 'so I did not have to pay baksheesh after all'. My grandfather had a special way of saying 'baksheesh' – with a sort of relish, with a smacking of the lips, as he was a little inclined to do when he ate!

My grandfather had thought over the plan of that hospital for so many years. In old age he still remembered the placing of every single stone. Architects from England were asked politely for plans but there was no chance of their getting his approval. The doctor fashioned his hospital himself as a craftsman, to serve the purpose of his profession and to suit the special needs of Aleppo. No outsider could possibly have had the same sensitivity, the special knowledge that he had.

Built of Aleppo stone, the plan was airy with large balconies and a garden, all surrounded by a strong wall and iron railings, making it look a little like a fortress. It was finished only three years before the outbreak of the 1914-18 war. The walnut doors and windows which all came on mule-back from a carpenter working in Maras – a three-day journey to the north – were reputedly carved by a German missionary called 'Herr Plank'. The pink-and-black marble which decorated the halls of polished yellow stone were from Aintab. Expert stonemasons came specially from Urfa. My grandfather was specially proud of the high stone skirting round the walls and up the stairs, built to withstand any amount of knocking about by stretchers and chairs being carried up and down. Visitors were asked to admire the lead caulking between each stone. Every time he went up and down his thin, blue-veined hands would absent-mindedly, lovingly, stroke along the sides with a little unconscious sigh of satisfaction. My grandfather had built a shrine and he thought of himself as a healer. The older inhabitants of Aleppo came close to worshipping him for more than human qualities. If Altounyan could not cure a person then no one could: 'He had his passport from Altounyan' – that was it.

This did not mean that my grandfather was not practical and modern. He was always eager to keep up with all the latest science – and to be one step ahead, if possible. As there was no mains water supply at the time the hospital was built, he took care to have a very efficient cistern built to collect the rainwater from the roof. Everyone who worked in the hospital remembers the strict rules about not stepping on the roof during the rainy season. He was always flexible and inventive in taking advantage of conditions as they were, and at the same time was ready to benefit from new inventions the moment they came along. Yearly journeys to Europe made certain that he kept up to date.

A visit to Europe was always good propaganda: the drive to the station, the grand procession of horses and carriages full of friends seeing him off; the return procession through the streets, the grooms and outriders, the new luggage (what had the doctor brought back this time?).

A dusty, tattered diary in a buttoned cover has survived to

chart those early years. It is dated 1908 (the year the foundations of the hospital were laid) but my grandfather scribbled in it all through the Great War to 1926, down to a few years after Ernest had come out to join him. Always distrustful of other people managing his money, in the diary he kept his private personal log for nearly twenty years. The charge for private visits was always one Turkish gold sovereign; night and urgent visits were five gold sovereigns. Sometimes he visited the same house five times in twenty-four hours. A weary scrawl says: 'four hours very hard work in the middle of the night twenty gold'. The richer the patients, the worse they were at paying but, when they did, 'PAID' would be stamped across the page. 'Sent account again but payment postponed till after the war', said another entry – perhaps the tin of butter received on 15 September 1914 made up for it. I imagine him pausing in the street outside a patient's house to write in his little book, silver-topped whip under one arm, horse pawing the ground, groom waiting with his medical case. Many of the names scribbled in that book three-quarters of a century ago are still remembered in Aleppo: Homsi, Hindie, Gazale, Poche, Sola, Marcoploli, still listed nostalgically by homesick Alepines, sometimes with the refrain 'and Altounyan saved his life'. In 1908, when Aleppo was still part of the Ottoman Empire, my grandfather's patients were 'Hawaja' or 'Agha' or 'Bey', sometimes even 'Pasha'. After 1914 we have the Germans ('Herr', 'Von', 'Baron'), and then the British ('Captain', 'Commander', 'His Excellency'). When Syria was under French mandate, my grandfather went on recording: 'Le Comte', 'Son Excellence', 'Monsieur'. Females usually appear attached to their men – so-and-so's daughter, wife, etc.

The money going out was recorded too: there are notes about the tiny sums paid to the maid, Arshalouis, or Nvart the nurse's salary ('two pounds a month'). And there are memoranda about money received towards the church he was planning to build in his wife's memory (Harriet died in 1907), pathetic little amounts from grateful patients, probably saved up piastre by piastre: 'one pound from Marie'; 'fifty piastres from Onnig', perhaps an orphan from the orphanage Harriet had started for destitute Armenian children.

The Unknown Remembered Gate

The stumpy little volume, all the way from London, was two-third adverts for such items as 'Alax pills' and 'Cascara Sagrada', an aromatic liqueur for the great complaint of modern times. 'Bivo Beef and Iron wine' was made by submitting choice lean to great pressure in the cold ('Of great use in nervous muscular prostration'). There was 'The Livingstone Rouser', a combination of rhubarb and quinine, or 'Forced March', a cola-nut compound extensively used by travellers, explorers and military men ('Allays thirst and hunger and sustains strength under mental and physical strain without subsequent depression'). Chloral and belladonna were recklessly prescribed to people of all ages. What did the Doctor Altounyan think of this? He used to scold his patients for taking even simple remedies like aspirin because it masked their symptoms.

He was still operating from the old Arab house when he went to England on yet another of his refresher visits. It was 1896, the year after the X-ray had been invented. My grandfather bought one. Back in Aleppo he called all society together in his drawing-room and gave a demonstration: 'I showed the skeletons of the visitor's hands, put metallic objects in closed wooden boxes showing them the way the rays penetrated through'. As newer models came out, the Aleppo Clinic kept pace. During World War I, Aleppo was the only city in the Ottoman Empire that had an X-ray machine. Needless to say, the courtiers at Constantinople were jealous: 'Send the X-ray to us at once', they demanded. So a collection of old wires, coils and burnt-out tubes were neatly packed and dispatched. Nothing more was heard, no questions asked, no instructions sent. Some months later, Jemal Pasha (later to be Commander-in-Chief of the Turkish Army) broke his leg near Aleppo and had to be X-rayed. 'You did quite right', was his comment when told the story. That is the prize of the Altounyan collection of pebble-stories. It is almost worn away with telling.

Jemal Pasha, who possessed the first car Aleppo had ever seen – it was bright red – was a frequent visitor to my grandfather's house. He was persuaded by my father's sister, Norah, to divert Army rations to feed little Armenian children who were wandering about everywhere in a most pitiful state, having lost their families in the massacres. Jemal Pasha (whose life was ended by an Armenian not very long after the war) was intelligent enough to see that the Armenian and his hospital were irreplaceable in that particular time and place. My grandfather's lifestyle convinced him that here was a man who thought of nothing but his profession and his patients, irrespective of politics. There was no mistaking that zest and extraordinary energy which allowed him to enjoy a simple thing like peeling a ripe peach but also gave him the stamina to carry through the most taxing and complicated surgical operation. Although Assadour's brother had recently been cut down in the streets of Bitlis in front of his family, he was able to put that aside and devote himself to his job. He never lost a certain childlike innocence and trust that the world is essentially a happy place. Everyone remembers him as a host telling Khoja Nasredin stories and perhaps adding one or two of his own about some of his more clownish patients – those, for instance, who boiled the prescription paper and drank the 'tea', instead of going to the chemist.

For all his cleverness, the miracle doctor could not prevent his wife dying of cancer in 1907, after almost twenty years of marriage. Their last summer together was spent in a little Irish village on the shores of Carlingford Loch. Harriet comes over as a brave but rather stern character. My father used to tell me how, on their Sunday drives back from church, she insisted on having the blinds tightly closed. The only portrait we have of her is of a Florence Nightingale figure in nurse's uniform, clasping a prayer book as she gazes into space, lips pursed. When she became suspicious that she was not being told the truth about her illness, she cross-questioned a young niece until she found out and then calmy accepted her fate. Though she tried to bring up her children to believe in God, legend has it that she died an agnostic. In Ireland, Assadour (or Theodore) is remembered as a 'darling man', but all agree that Harriet was a puzzle though she was said to have a certain dry sense of humour. She is much less real to me than Assadour's mother who lives on as a warm look in the eyes of her son. Neither my father nor his sister ever talked to us about their mother. After all, they were both sent away at a very early age.

Norah was sent to school in England, like her brother, and shared some of his Bloomsbury life. The Royal Academician Roger Fry painted her portrait. She positively enjoyed being what her brother would call a 'mongrel', and told me what fun it was to be able to see both sides. It was impossible to call her pretty, as she had her father's looks, but somehow she managed to be feminine nevertheless. I shall never forget her mischievous laugh and the chic way she dressed. She married a French diplomat and lead what seemed to us a glamorous life, flying to romantic places like Bangkok and Kabul. Secretly, I resolved to grow up like her. After her mother's death and all through World War I, she lived in Aleppo as my grandfather's partner and support. She died in the same year as her father and was missed by everyone because she had the gift of making us see the positive side of being what we were. She balanced Ernest's unhappiness and probably understood him better than anyone.

I do not know if my grandfather ever saw his mother again after he left Sivas with his doctor cousin to go to Aintab. Of course, he may have slipped back after he returned from America, but it would have been a long and difficult journey, probably on horseback, with every chance of being robbed again. Once he had settled in Aleppo, there was no one he could leave in charge. His status depended on his personality. He had neither much land nor old family tradition, which counted for so much in Aleppo, but he became an 'honorary notable' because he was what the town needed at the time: someone who was not too tightly connected with any of the communities. He soon realized that his reputation and his life must depend on being slightly apart – and very clever. My father once summoned up the courage to ask his father how on earth he had managed to carry on working for and treating as friends the people who had murdered his brother and possibly the rest of his family. The old man admitted that there had been a moment when he had thought of cutting down a Turk, in revenge for his brother, and then committing suicide. But a violent and obstinate anger had welled up after the first shock of grief – a determination to live the rest of his life as fully as possible 'and show them'.

Once a year at Easter, Black Grandpa stood up in the pulpit

of the Protestant church he had built in memory of his wife and delivered a sort of sermon on health and morals. I have them all stacked in a brown heap. The writing is his careful Armenian script but the words are Turkish. Many of his sayings were remembered for a long time and quoted to the next generation – *and* the next.

Chapter Two

AND THE Collingwoods? Where does the story of a family begin? Anthropologists would say that we are all descended from seven women from the upper reaches of the Nile in Africa; the genealogist has to stop when the church records and the tombstones give out; the biographer picks over the generations, choosing a piece here, a dark scrap there, to make a collage. The Altounyans did not leave many traces. Graves, especially in Armenian villages, were often unmarked and, after the deportations, soon became lost. Black Grandpa's travelling inkpots, his anatomy notebooks and a few of his other possessions have come down to me, but he was not fond of writing letters just for the fun of it.

The Collingwoods were letter-writers and diarists. However, they were not always as revealing as they might have been. Great-grandfather William left six black-bound volumes – 'diaries' he called them. They record what he considered important (family events, including his own birth) but on the very first page is a warning to anyone seeking personal anecdotes. There are sheaves of letters preserved but, now and then, my mother mentions 'having a good clear-out at Lanehead' – making bonfires.

William Collingwood, my great-grandfather, and a member of the Royal Watercolour Society, a few of whose pictures can be found in the Victoria and Albert Museum, was born in 1819 and died in 1903. The family home was in Greenwich. His father was an architect. His grandfather was Samuel the Printer for nearly fifty years at the Clarendon Press, Oxford. Samuel had a large family from three of his four wives, three of whom he outlived. Though he had so many children already, he took William's elder brother (another Samuel) off his son's hands and brought him up as his own. Queen Victoria visited his press and was pleased to print her name on a piece of blue silk – in gold. His grave is under a yew tree in St Giles' churchyard in Oxford, which is now a busy traffic island.

William inherited the drawing talent but, with it, the 'unconventional and independent character' which is also a family trait. At school he was a prodigy in Greek and Latin though very backward in mathematics. The impediment to an academic career was that at an early age he had doubts about the Thirty-Nine Articles or doctrines of the Church of England (as one would expect from one who was to become a pillar of the Plymouth Brethren). Anyone accepting a scholarship at a university had to sign the Test Act or promise to follow the established church, although in 1828, by the time he was fifteen, the Act was partially repealed. (It was to be completely abolished in the universities by the time his son Gershom was ready to go, in the early 1870s.) He was therefore put into business, although it was well known that the Collingwoods did not shine in this field. Luckily for him, the business was Ackermann's, a famous purveyor of artists' materials, then in the Strand. A family friend in the firm got the boy a 'live-in' apprenticeship. He spent his evenings, when he was not walking the five miles back home to Greenwich at weekends, in drawing 'copies' for Ackermann, encouraged by a motherly housekeeper, and very soon the boy's outstanding talent was noticed by another family friend who bought him free of his apprenticeship. In 1837, William set up as a freelance artist in Hastings.

Hardly had he 'put a couple of sketches in a shop window, sold one for fifteen shillings' than along came the artist Samuel Prout who began a lifelong friendship by immediately finding him pupils. At nineteen, William was teaching with success and was accepted in a number of noble families whose ladies made much of him.

While sketching on the shore one day he was 'found out' by a rich amateur artist called John Henry Maw who exhibited at the Royal Academy and had a house full of pictures. This man's main claim to fame was that he had 'disputed with Ruskin about the laws of perspective'. At the time he met William he was employing no less a person than J.S. Cotman to teach his three children watercolour painting. Mr Maw was proud of his Elizabethan style drawing-room and wanted his new protégé to paint his portrait in it, dressed as a cavalier 'with a hawk and his rapier and so forth'. However, William found that working all the time in dark corners, as he had to do for Mr Maw, was a strain on his eyesight, 'so he abandoned it for out-of-door landscape'.

A chance meeting with yet another London friend led William to Liverpool, which became his home for the next forty-five years. Records for 1838 have him down as 'artist' and 'Professor of drawing'.

Before he went to the Lake District from Liverpool, William had never seen mountains but as a boy he had copied the ice-patterns on his window because he imagined they looked like the Swiss Alps; a quarter of a century later, 'Circumstances drew him to the Alps – and altered his life'. In 1851, a young Swiss girl called Maria Imhoff, from the town of Arbon on the southern shores of Lake Constance, came to stay with friends of the Collingwoods in order to visit the Great Exhibition. William and Maria were married in 1853 and, from then on, two out of every three years were spent in Switzerland. Like the Altounyans, the children were brought up to be familiar with two countries and were used to the idea of speaking different languages at home. Familiarity with Swiss scenery was a great asset to William in those pre-abstract days when an artist had to find 'subjects' to make into pictures. The next generation still had the same problem. My White Grandpa wrote that 'a good deal of our favourite places are spoilt with woodcutting so one is pushed into things not sketched before'. Many years later when my mother Dora went out to Syria I was not surprised to find her writing to her father Gershom: 'I'm afraid you would find nothing to paint round here. The hills are low and bare and there is no scenery at all . . . but if you walk a quarter of a mile behind the house you can see mountains with snow on fifty miles away – quite good crinkly shapes.'

At first, William's drawings of unfamiliar mountains were

hard and 'unsentimental' (meaning, in those days, that they had no feeling) but, on his honeymoon, he 'saw the dawn blush of light on the Jungfrau and its reflection in a little tarn. This stirred him greatly.' This picture got a mention – if critical – in John Ruskin's Academy notes (*c.* 1854):

> Striking in effect, an attractive picture but sadly wanting in accuracy and detail. If the artist study the mountain carefully ... he might produce a valuable picture.

The 'Professor' (as Ruskin was known) liked to make a distinction between the artists he approved of, who had the intention at least to be true to nature, and those he 'abhorred', who aimed only at being 'pretty and clever'. William did not 'dispute' with the great man but went and tried again. The next year he produced an accurate and beautiful watercolour of the Matterhorn and the Theodule glacier below it. From this time on Mr Ruskin was pleased to buy Collingwoods, saying he liked them because 'they were done wet'. The two men became friends.

Like other Collingwoods, William did not find his facility in drawing and painting enough to fill his life. As he got older he spent more and more of his energies on the Evangelical creed he had adopted. He wrote many pamphlets on the Plymouth Brethren and very nearly became a missionary in China. But he never felt that painting was incompatible with his religious duties. For him, appreciating mountain landscape and other forms of nature was a form of worship. But his beliefs did make him resign from the New Watercolour Society, later the Royal Institute, when life insurance was demanded of members in 1845. He thought this implied a mistrust of Providence.

Gershom was the eldest of William's three children. His name means 'a stranger in a strange land' (did Maria long for her Swiss mountains and compare them sadly with the Cumbrian fells?). He was born in 1854 in Liverpool which he tended to despise ('You cannot keep up to scratch in a place like Liverpool'). Far away in the central plateau of Anatolia another boy was born in the same year (if you can believe any of Black Grandpa's many passports which gave him three or four years leeway – convenient for adding or subtracting a year or two according to who you wish to impress).

Gershom's early letters to his 'Dear Papa' show a certain quaintness – a finicky obsession for getting things right: 'David is not much better, not much worse – about middling', 'Eliza is pretty well – not very'. A rough crossing from Folkstone is described with a careful map to demonstrate the position of the boat and the direction of the wind, explaining why he did not feel seasick. *Murray's Guide* had deceived them twice: 'left four miles out of the journey, and described the people in the hotel as "uncivil" when they were not so.' 'Climbing the Swiss mountains is like going up stairs for four hours' (Gershom would never have described walking up his beloved fells so). The Collingwoods tended to avoid the exaggeration and conversational flourishes which my father so enjoyed.

Gershom spent his fifteenth birthday (6 August 1869) with his father, walking and sketching near Mont Blanc. 'Papa lost his small red pencil ... he did not like going up so the guide held out his alpenstock like a rail.' Born and bred in Greenwich, 'Papa' was no climber and could not compete with his half German–Swiss son. But they breakfasted happily enough on snow and brandy. Gershom wrote teasingly to his mother that he had been wearing the same collar for a month, 'every day – all the time'. Maria died of consumption in 1873 many years before William, when not yet fifty: 'Mama's chest is more affected than was thought.' She is begged not to waste her strength on long letters. She remains a shadowy figure to me, like most great-grandparents are when not given to writing letters.

Even as a boy, Gershom spent all the time he could at Windermere where he thought himself 'a deal more at home than in Liverpool': 'Do you think I could use some of the £5 you sent me to go to Windermere?'; 'I am glad to be near fells again and have made a few trips to the heights. One gets the mountain feel with a wonderful swiftness after leaving Coniston behind'; 'The stars are much brighter here than in Liverpool. The snow mountains reflected in the English lakes are as good as those Italian lakes, though you may doubt it'. On 13 April 1871, when he was nearly seventeen, he walked for the first time from Gillhead, on the eastern shores of Windermere, up to the top of Coniston Old Man:

> Walked to Coniston Old Man. After a breakfast of syrup vulgarly called treacle. Rowed across the lake (Windermere). Icy. Then across Esthwait Water to Hawkshead. Then I saw the Old Gentleman who was wearing a white hat and asserted his gentlemanly origin by pulling it off to me. I went past the Copper Mines and was soon out of reach of houses and suchlike abominations. There was a blue haze which spoilt the view from the top – but the near peaks were glorious. I refreshed myself with snow and by 12 of Greenwich time precisely I got up on the cairn and yelled 'hip hip hurrah' as I had promised. But the Gillhead people neither heard nor saw me.

A hundred years later, his great-grandchildren still take their new babies up the mountain to ask for the 'Old Man's' blessing.

In 1872, Gershom went to Oxford University. He was 'plagued' by the non-arrival of his piano and the obligation to answer so many letters in German from relatives ('Bad enough to get them'). He was chronically short of money ('Please remember the poor') and his coat looked more shabby than it did at home because 'one must always be straight and tidy here'. Asked to show some ladies round the colleges he realized afterwards that he had had holes in his trousers. His rooms were damp and on the ground floor, his friends dropped in all the time so that he could not settle down to work till near midnight. 'Papa' wrote long letters, complaining of his son's reticence. He got the reply that, not being used to putting down all his thoughts on paper, he did not see the wrongness of such reticence. Gershom was eighteen, obviously fighting for independence as fiercely as his father had done at the same age: 'Pray do not think me ritualistic for dating my letter "Advent Sunday" . . . You condemn utterly the use of instruments in worship, I *like* instruments and find it more religious to hear Mr Hallé than to go to a service at New. I like chanting very much'; 'I'm afraid you will be shocked at my going to chapel but it is nice and quiet and a pleasant way of beginning the day'. He felt at home in Oxford: 'I can go anywhere and do anything I please without any trouble ... Everyone is obliged to be civil to varsity men'.

But Papa had furnished Gershom with a most valuable introduction to Ruskin and he meant to use it, in spite of the fact that his tutor assured him that Mr Ruskin would not do him any good. By the time he had taken his degree, he was told, he would no longer want to be an artist. His first meeting with Ruskin was on 26 October 1872:

> I told him I wanted to be an artist and he said he didn't know how he could help me ... in the end he said I could come to his drawing classes if I was tired of reading or if it was wet. He is having his place fitted up very comfortably so as to be a quiet drawing place for students. He will be there when not preparing for his lectures. He will look over what I am doing.

Gershom said he was reading for Honours and the old man warned him that he would do himself no good. 'I was to tell my tutor from him that it was bad for my constitution,' but 'he laughed a good deal and I like him very much. He dresses in the most extraordinary way, but he is not in the least unpleasant.' As they parted 'He compared me to a compass needle. I would find some attraction one way or another.'

Although he had so little money, Gershom bought three rugs to cheer his rooms, 'one a little Persian and one Indian of splendid colour'. His father was tempted by another, 'got from refugees, ten or a dozen foot square, two hundred years old, costing £5.1.5'. It was a pity neither of them journeyed to Aleppo to see Black Grandpa's room full of rugs – one silk, said by T.E. Lawrence to be worth 'the sack of Aleppo'. Gershom always wrote at a table covered with a Persian carpet, perhaps one he bought as a student in Oxford.

The 'compass' veered about for some time more. Gershom did try to please his father, who was anxious his son should have the benefits of Oxford that he had missed. He won a scholarship for £130 and, in 1876, he obtained a first in philosophy. But when it came to trying for a fellowship, his way seemed to be blocked: 'Thanks for the £10, this fellowship hunting can be expensive'. Perhaps he had not the right church-going habits or was too outspoken to the wrong people. 'Masters like his style but he does not seem to know much. If only he would settle to reading,' his tutor wrote to William.

Gershom soon abandoned the idea of obtaining a fellowship. That same year, at the Slade, he began to 'paint as if he meant it' and found it 'really fine being an artist all day'. He exhibited in galleries, including the Academy, and gave his water-colourist father instruction in oil painting 'which has a great advantage over watercolour': 'White – that blessed colour – can often mix colours to get a more delicate tint'. He kindly set out a pallet for 'beginners', advocating 'clean solid lights and clear warm darks'. But commissions were slow in coming: 'Most people I know want commissions themselves'. He found the art examinations puerile. As he said, he had 'passed in freehand when a baby'; 'I am promoted to life without any solicitation. Am loath to leave the antique which is easier and more beautiful'. It was all too easy. Nothing to get his teeth into. 'At present taste execution is everything, composition no account.'

Ruskin kept his eye on the promising young man. He came to tea in his flat in London with a bundle of his latest drawings from Venice. 'He is very well and had done some jolly things'; 'Must read "Stones of Venice"'. Ruskin gave Gershom a Greek translation to do and asked him to Brantwood to work on it: 'Mr R. was going to the Continent but was so delighted with the idea that he decided to stay at home. The dear old man was quite affectionate. He already glowingly anticipates the beginning of July.' 'For such a gorgeous turnout of a plough as this one cannot draw back one's hand', he wrote to his father. When the month of July brought rain to Coniston and Brantwood, as it usually does, Ruskin saw it as a punishment for sin. Gershom planned a translation of the works of Herodotus: 'fifty quaint stories and fifty dainty etchings at a guinea each'.

Gershom seems to have been on friendly terms with the artist Burne-Jones. He frequently borrowed money from him. He had painting lessons from him and was encouraged by the older man. Sometimes he dined at his home: 'very quiet dinner. They don't affect "high life" and he receives company in a blue shirt and red tie. He seems a very nice man . . .' Gershom was obviously rather proud of his friendship and told his father, 'I was strolling along the street the other day and some one grasped my wrist, he [Burne-Jones] had come out to post a letter'.

But the compass was still wobbling.

Gershom began to get painful boils on his face, and his stomach was giving him trouble, 'being in an awful mess'. Doctors advised him to abstain from drinking and smoking, and to take long walks. His friends advocated champagne and brought him a bottle: 'I don't feel a bit better for that glassful. I wish I could put my head on your lap and sleep there,' he wrote to his future wife.

He had met Edith Mary Isaac, the elder daughter of the six children of Thomas Isaac of Maldon, Essex, at his uncle's house in London when she was attending a boarding school run by her aunt, Mrs Georgina Isaac, and her very good friend, Mrs Samuel Collingwood. In 1875, at the age of eighteen, she was allowed to study art in London.

In her early years, the little girl, who was her father's favourite and went on his business rounds with him, had lived a boyish life, playing among her father's wharfs and granaries. When the boys went to boarding school, she expected to go with them and she was horrified to find herself among a lot of girls. Luckily for her, it was considered a rather modern school for those times, with exercise for the girls in the fresh air, such as a walk between breakfast and lessons. Every other week there was a party for brothers and cousins. Gershom thought he could count himself as a cousin sometimes and signed himself so in his letters to her. He was a few years older than her and at first inclined to be patronizing, changing her name to 'Dorrie' and giving her brotherly advice: 'Dear Miss Isaac you ought to see how pictures are hung before sending anything in. Don't forget about hanging a label over the front attached by a nail to the back.' He even asked her to meet Mr Ruskin when he came to tea. Miss Isaac responded gracefully. And he answered, 'Dear Edith, many thanks for the apple blossom which will be of great use to me. I am now at work on it. There is only one petal lost, the leaves are perfect and the flowers fresh.' In no time it was

'Darling Dorrie . . . My picture is in the Academy. Aren't you glad? Your Gershom.'

But William would not let them get engaged. Not surprisingly, he didn't see that his son had any prospects. Gershom wrote: 'We must make an effort to be happy without being certificated sweethearts with a diploma from friends and relations including everybody and signed by Mrs Grundy as Home Secretary. We may always love each other but we may never live together. Meanwhile I must work hard and you will come and see me when you go for a walk sometimes – and I will come and see you – tomorrow night.' Passionate letters were exchanged, sometimes every hour. Coming in late, Gershom would grope for them off the doormat in the dark. 'We are one candle lighted from the other,' he wrote. 'Not the sun and the moon as you said because the moon would go out if the sun did.'

Gershom and 'Dorrie' were to feel equal partners in their marriage more than was usual at that period: both of them contributed to the family purse, with the help of the skill they shared. Now they set about trying to 'create confidence' in their parents: 'All we can do is to live as tidily as possible'. Apparently, they were restricted as to correspondence because they had to get someone else to address envelopes so that their handwriting would not be recognized. It was hard.

Mr Ruskin saw what was happening and 'called' the young man to help him study the geology of Coniston. In his spare time he helped build a pier for the Brantwood boat *Jumping Jenny*. Then, in 1882, Gershom went abroad with Ruskin, filling sketchbooks with French and Italian sculpture in between studying the geology of the Savoy Alps. When they got back, 'Papa' had been persuaded to approve an engagement. The couple were married at Kensington Registry Office in 1883.

It was typical of my grandparents' life that they had to delay their honeymoon a little because Gershom was required by Mr Ruskin to do some copies of Turners for an imminent lecture. The actual date of the wedding was decided after they had acquired a cottage at Gillhead which was to become almost as 'hallowed' as Coniston. This was a little hamlet on the east shore of Windermere where Gershom and his brother and sister used to spend holidays with their old nurse Harriet and her husband, William Alexander, who was a commercial fisherman. He used often to entertain the young people with traditional folk-tales, like an ancient Norse Skald: tales of fights with the Scots, the doings of the monks of Furness Abbey, or the giant of Troutbeck, or the fearsome 'boggle' or ghost who haunted the roads on a Saturday night and drove befuddled revellers out of their wits. These stories gave young Gershom his first interest in Norse names in his adopted Lake District, suggesting to him the story of Thorstein, the Viking's son, who explored the river up from Greenodd where his father had settled, and discovered the great unknown lake at Coniston sometimes called Thurston Water. In 1897 (just three years before Ruskin died) Gershom, after he had been working on a translation from Icelandic, went on a three-month visit to Iceland to sketch the sites of the classic Norse legends. He took with him a strand of 'Dorrie's' hair, plaited as a watchchain, to keep off the evil eye, and the speedwell and the forget-me-not from Lanehead in his buttonhole. His first letter home was to his eight-year-old son Robin: 'My dearest Bobbin'. He was on a Danish boat so they said 'Bort and Steerbord'; 'The Danish sailors are rather like inferior English – but no doubt they are nailing good men at the job . . . I would like to have you all with me if I was sure of not seeing you seasick'. The fifteen letters are mostly to 'Molly', as 'Dorrie' seems to have been called later. A few to each of the children were carefully aimed at what would interest each of them particularly.

All the four children, Dora, Barbara, Robin and Ursula, were born at Gillhead. Dora was barely five when the family moved to Lanehead on Coniston in 1891 because it was only a mile down the road from Brantwood which Ruskin had bought as a tumbledown house, without even visiting it, because of the fine views promised. That year they spent Christmas in their new house and New Year at Brantwood. In that year, Gershom wrote *The Life and Work of John Ruskin*. It is still the standard biography.

As he got to know Ruskin better, he began to realize his complex personality and how much the older man had come to depend on him, especially towards the end of his life. One sentence in a letter to 'Papa' – 'one of the greatest disappointments I have ever had' – seems to allude to Ruskin. It is not clear whether the 'disappointment' was Ruskin's loss of faith or his dependence on laudanum. The letter goes on: 'I make no doubt that the continual grumbling and looking at the bad of things and their incurableness has to some extent warped Mr R's mind lately. Most people say he is mad. I know that on many points he is more sensible than most of us. He has lost faith in Christianity and one cannot tell how far. He declares he delights in puzzling people and he puzzles me. He has lots of spiritual advisers with condemnation in their white ties . . . Mr R is not very well he has been dabbling in spiritualism again. He talks of seeing ghosts and getting news from the spiritual world.'

For nine years Brantwood was the background for life at Lanehead and it was a busy and exciting time. My grandmother kept up her music and her painting in spite of her large family. She did not seem to miss the seascapes and open skies of her native Essex, although she always fetched her cooks and housemaids from Maldon. She specialized in flower paintings and miniature portraits on ivory of the rich ladies living in the great houses round the lakes. She also did sensitive watercolours of her husband's beloved lakes and mountains. Everything she did found a ready sale and she sometimes earned more than her husband. As well as this, she travelled abroad every year and brought back sheaves of landscapes which sold well. Money was always tight and it was never certain whether they would be able to stay at Lanehead after the current lease ran out, although Miss Holt, heiress of the Blue Funnel Line in Liverpool, was a good and generous friend and admirer of the family. There were many who must have envied the Collingwoods their energy, charm and skills. Although no one would have called the family Bohemian, there was a certain zest to their lifestyle which was attractive.

The rambling house, with its attics, lofts and cellars, its large garden with rhododendron thickets which made such good 'houses', and tall pines – watchtowers to be climbed to see the lake and the mountains – was ideal for the four children. They had regular lessons with their father and were often employed as models for pictures (at a penny an hour). But most of the time they were free and could live their own lives, out of sight of their parents, if they wished, yet safe. They painted and drew almost from the moment they could hold pencils; they edited the family magazine, 'Nothing Much', which saw the first 'publication' of some of their father's articles; they published tiny books, a few inches square; they ran a secret club whose motto was 'Run and find out' and whose greeting sign was 'Good hunting'. When my mother, Dora, was having to teach all of us in Syria, she was astonished to find what a lot still lurked in the corners of her mind: 'We must have been pretty well taught. I wish my children had the advantages I had.' No wonder she despaired at my spelling: 'But my dear, you must not spell all right "alright", you really mustn't. Do you do it on purpose or as a protest against convention? It looks vulgar (if that means anything to you) like drinking with your mouth full, or saying "excuse me" when you hiccup . . . As to your spelling as a whole, heaven help you, evidently your teachers can't.'

Though they could not afford to travel much, the young Dora and Barbara went in turn to stay with the Austrian–Swiss branch of the family. Dora's letters home show a vivaciousness which I hardly recognize in my mother who was quiet and slightly withdrawn and who never could quite imagine how she had come to be the mother of five. The first thing she did when away from her family was to have her hair cut ('I'm sure it is very good for me'). I don't know if she ever did it again. She appreciated a new violinist called Kuberlic ('the name sounds like water under a boat'). Single-handed she defended her Queen about the Boer War ('We didn't begin it, did we Daddy?'). A 'most dreadfully lively girl', with a krugerrand hung round her neck on a chain, knocked her down over the argument, 'just before dinner too, when I had done my hair'. Another time she was 'nearly throttled' for displaying a picture of Buller above her bed. Press cuttings from Daddy at Lanehead provided her with ammunition.

The Swiss uncles seem to have been paper merchants because Dora wrote of playing with the huge rolls of paper in the mill. The life was as different as possible from Presbyterian, hardworking Lanehead – 'It is gaudy. I gloat, I gloat' – the huge meals with lobsters and champagne, the old men 'who ate with their knives and laughed loudly', the ladies who overdressed in such ugly colours, the boisterous uncles who waltzed her round and played practical jokes, the sledge rides, the excitement of being treated as a grown-up young lady. She was taken aback by the way they asked her opinion about anything the least bit 'artistic', such as choosing silk for a dress, embroidery patterns or a frame for a picture. 'It is very odd the way they ask my advice about everything and take it in the most ridiculous manner.' She did not think much of the art teaching. A Herr G. was engaged to teach them German and arithmetic and 'to explain Egyptian art'. He thought her drawing of a Virginia creeper very good, 'but I don't think he knows much about it because it is *very bad*'. Through all the excitement she never forgot her career. It might be 'wildly exciting' to let herself be electrified, to observe coloured lights inside airtight glass tubes, to learn about the phases of the moon, what the Gulf Stream really was, and to read Froissart (in French), to understand a sermon about China in German, how to mend a bicycle tyre with a solution of rubber and turpentine, to shoot with a gun and hit the target, to learn to ski. But . . . 'My comb by the way has lost twenty teeth all at once so I have bought another one of the new electric kind called "Goliath". My green dress has had to be let out two inches in all directions.' Life was still real and in earnest. She gave English lessons to her cousins out of *Little Black Sambo*, 'one tiger a day'. Barbara got scolded for spelling their German address wrong: 'Your writing slightly shocks the family here, especially the outside of the envelope. You must not write on the *address* side of cards.' Bad writing was one of the things my mother always considered 'vulgar'. She and Barbara wrote beautifully. White Grandpa's – Gershom's – hand was as if a fly had fallen into the inkpot and was making its way across the paper. He himself called it 'chameleon' writing. All of us five children, except Mavis, developed an almost unreadable hand.

Part of Dora's mind never left Lanehead, never stopped thinking about 'getting on' with her painting: 'Mother you promised to write me *everything* [twice underlined] Daddy said about my drawings and I have not had a single word about it.

Please write me soon, before you forget, because I rather extra particularly want to know and it is rather important to me.'

When Robin was born, Gershom hoped fervently that he would win scholarships. The only boy in the family had to be properly educated – sent to school. The girls did not matter. When the telegram came offering him a scholarship to Rugby, Robin was in the bath. The whole family lined up on the stairs, waiting for him to come out and open it.

'Pebble-stories' about my uncle's childhood are as startling as Black Grandpa's! Apparently, he never needed to be taught anything. He invented the whole of Euclid for himself when he was three, perhaps Pythagoras as well! He nearly killed himself trying to make gunpowder: 'I consider that a most satisfactory explosion', he is reported to have said, picking himself up after being blown across the room! He remembered the exact spot in his father's study where, at the age of seven, the conviction that he was going to be a philosopher fell on him 'like a cloak'. Before he was five he was helping his father with his novel, *Thorstein of the Mere*, which was published in 1895:

> Thorstein is yours, you made him yours
> A writer asks no finer flattery
> Than five-year-old's assault and battery.
> You seize the copy and revise
> Absorbed the proofs, devoured the pages . . .
> Thanks Robin.

Thorstein was written 'for a little boy . . . meant as a picture of his home as it might have been a thousand years ago'. The dialect 'should be familiar to a properly brought up child of these parts'. In fact, expressions like 'cruddle', 'flitter' and 'as wankle as a wet sark' are not so difficult to guess at. They add exotic encrustation to the text. There may be a 'world of antiquarian knowledge behind each sentence', as some bedazzled reviewer put it, but there is much feeling as well, as in 'awful edges of mountain rolling and plunging along the skyline as wheels that move' and Thorstein's first view of his lake, 'the huge fells tossing like breakers on a stormy beach and rolling away and afar like the heaving waves of the sea'. Long before

Arthur Ransome discovered it, Gershom had described Peel Island, in the midst of Thurston Water, as 'lying all alone like a little ship at anchor, while all the mere moves up-bank and down-bank as the wind maybe'.

Robin, born in 1889, became more 'famous' than other Altounyans or Collingwoods. His subject was mainly philosophy and the history of Roman Britain. His book *Aspects of Art* and a mass of drawings show that he could equally well have been an artist. His book about Roman Britain has only recently been superseded as a textbook. Like many of the Collingwoods, notably Great-Grandfather William, he seems to have been an intellectual with a very strong artistic bent. My mother was a little surprised to find his name in a list of subscribers to the surrealists. I don't think *she* ever considered them seriously.

John Ruskin died on the 20 January 1990 and Queen Victoria in 1901, and this brought changes for William Gershom Collingwood and his family. Dora, aged thirteen, could not remember a time when Mr Ruskin had not been present in the background of life at Lanehead, like a super ancestor or demigod. Luckily, she had decided to keep a diary that year. 'Mr Ruskin died at half past three today', she wrote. 'Mother counted ninety wreaths but there were many more. There was one of primroses and even of daffodils! If only we had not got the influenza we could have seen them.' And at Brantwood they had 'the flue there bad' and could not have any visitors. No one came to Lanehead either, 'but Daddy was in the village all day meeting trains and finding rooms for people, and Mother was at Brantwood'. As soon as they were over 'the flue [*sic*]' my mother and her sister Barbara went to the village to get particulars on the relief of Ladysmith ('only we found *she* had not been relieved and so there were no particulars'). Of course, they went into the churchyard to see the remains of the wreaths, by then about three weeks old, but still recognizable: 'A great many wreaths and some had been very beautiful'. On 8 February, Mr Ruskin's birthday, they took another wreath, made of bay branches. 'We took *Modern Painters* to the Institute as a kind of birthday present – and my goodness, wasn't it heavy!' A few weeks later, 'Daddy' had designed the cross which was to be Ruskin's headstone. They showed it to Lily

Severn, a relation of Ruskin's, who exclaimed, 'What a wonderful man that little father of yours is, isn't he?'. 'It will be carved in very flat relief in the hard stone of the mountains here, so that yankees won't be able to take home chunks of "Ruskin's tomb" as Daddy said.' A few weeks later, the three of them went to the village again. In the churchyard, 'Daddy found a bit of wild olive on the ground which had evidently dropped out of a wreath – he brought it home to copy "The Crown of Wild Olive" from on the cross.' About twenty years later, Dora was to see her first olive trees from the train on her way to Aleppo, and she always loved painting them. That piece lying on the grave in Coniston must have come from some Mediterranean shore.

After Ruskin had died, my grandfather was for a time, from 1905, head of the Art Department at Reading University. The whole family moved to Reading in term time. Dora and Barbara qualified as art teachers there, in 1909, but their father's opinion still counted most: 'Pater says my perspective is wrong and painting coarse. This means I have wasted a whole term's work'. But, during their walks along the Thames at Reading, or up the paths to the moors above Lanehead, he 'made me feel so enthusiastic. I am going to work hard all the summer'. When my grandfather was at Reading he brought in certain innovations to the art syllabus. The entrance exam dropped arithmetic and essay – Dora was sorry about the essay: 'It is a means of communicating with the lecturer and we shall miss it'. Her essays were far better than Barbara's, though she always got in a panic in exams. Some years she won prizes for drawing and painting but there were periods of despair when 'perhaps I shall take up metal work and stop painting silly pictures that don't get hung'. A beaten copper rose bowl and a silver icon of the virgin and child show that she did just that. Like all Collingwoods she was a craftsman and could turn her hand to anything from packing up a parcel properly to improvising a fancy dress, though she was not particularly good at sewing – just went for the general effect, just as in the kitchen she hardly ever used recipes.

I was surprised to find my mother writing to Barbara: 'I don't know, I have always felt that the Collingwoods were lacking in something, some vitamin necessary for complete success in life, causing inability to take opportunities. Perhaps lack of perspicacity in choosing what horse to back is part of it.' One of my father's favourite words for feeling on top of the world was 'vitaminy'. Reading University was the outside world. The family must have benefited from a new environment, away from Coniston, where they were all under constant observation.

It was fashionable at the art school for everyone to be mildly in love all the time – even 'Pater': 'We are all more or less gone on . . . Pater came home quite in love with . . .' Dora struggled with a more serious crush for one of her woman teachers which she confides to her diary: 'I am a fool. I am a fool. I love her more and more.' This was natural in a girl of eighteen, but touching for me to watch her trying to contain a passion which was obviously almost more than she could manage: 'She is a very strong personality and a powerful character, very attractive to a weak character like myself'. After about a year she was still in thrall: 'I like her ever so much more than I did before but in a saner way . . . I can't think why I cannot be content with life without desire . . . On Sunday I made a vow to try and think less about the unobtainable. But how charming she looked pulling at the oars like a man, black curls flying.' The interesting thing is that 'Oriane' was Jewish. In the diary is a startling conversation between her and Dora about being Jewish. Dora writes: 'We have a great deal of Hebrew blood in our veins, though I am thankful to say our ancestors changed their religion a hundred and fifty years ago.' True, her mother's maiden name was Isaac, but this was no proof. While we lived in Jerusalem my mother was often taken for a Jewess, but that was because she did not look like a typical British memsahib. Uncle Robin certainly had a Hebrew look. He was thought to take after his mother. Like so many other families in England, we can trace our descent from Cromwell – 'in the female line' as mother always emphasized. It is fun to speculate that perhaps an Isaac daughter may have changed her religion when she married a Cromwell. It is well known that the Protector encouraged weavers and other craftsmen to come to East Anglia from the Netherlands and many of them were Jewish.

The Unknown Remembered Gate

Perhaps it was because they were a mixture of nationalities that the Collingwoods and the Altounyans needed a magnetic point to steady them wherever they were. For both families this was Lanehead. Though the Collingwoods enjoyed the amenities of Reading University they always longed to go north. My mother's diary, written at the beginning of one summer holiday when she and Barbara were to be alone together in the house, is lyrical: 'We haven't ordered any meat till Pater comes and are living on garden produce. An ideal life, we two alone in the garden with no neighbours, to come and go as we like, hatless and gloveless in our oldest clothes. We haven't done any work. Greek testament doesn't count because unnecessary. Work can wait till we get over the delight of being home.' Under the four firs at the end of the lawn there was no noise except for 'squirrels cracking nuts in the trees and a cart in the distance carrying bracken. Across the lake the church clock striking'. When Robin was home they went on the lake, sometimes sailing by starlight 'with the village lights reflected in the lake and the owls hooting'. On one occasion, Dora tried to paint the aurora borealis reflected in the water. Beside her Robin was fiddling to get his very first pipe alight. As in *Thorstein*, 'it seemed that all the heavens were aflame and the very mountains themselves were blazing. Great sheets of wavering flame turned blood colour and the sky between them was green, and the stars faded away. Then it throbbed and shifted and changed like clouds at sunset though the sun itself was long gone down and there was no moon ... They saw one another pale as grass in the firelight.'

Though she was apparently absorbed in her career, Dora was aware of her advancing age. She was nearly thirty. She would soon be 'on the shelf'. Her mother 'Molly', or 'Dorrie' as the girls usually called her (she was more like a big sister and sometimes even a younger sister) was capable of embarrassing 'howlers': 'Really for a sensible person Molly does do the oddest things'. All she had done was to enquire of one of Dora's partners at a dance – *in her presence* – when he was going to get married. 'I felt myself going scarlet, I did not dare look at Mr B. Pater said something quickly. He mentioned the incident at breakfast this morning. Said he had woken up at night and thought of it in horror. So did I. She is so innocent that she hadn't even noticed the DOUBLE ONGTONG.'

Dora was quite certain that she did not want to marry Arthur Ransome. 'The other day Mrs M. asked mother if it was true that it was Miss Collingwood that Mr Ransome is after. This is not the first or the second time. I don't wonder,' confided Dora to her diary, a lot of which was in a code which still keeps its secret, 'that the neighbours talk about Arthur and us, and I equally don't care.' From his very first visit, Arthur had made himself part of the family and proceeded to soak up any spare emotional energy the Collingwoods had left. His appearances were always theatrical, as the first one when my grandfather found him lying spread-eagled on a flat rock in the middle of a rushing river. 'Are you alive young man?' he called across the water. From that first meeting Arthur Ransome declared his 'most frantic approval' of my grandfather, whom he called 'The Scald' because he looked like a Swedish bard. He could hardly believe his luck when he was allowed to call my grandmother 'Aunt' and she trusted him to do shopping for her in the village. The Collingwoods grew to accept him as an adopted relative. He was always turning up unexpectedly: 'The sound of a boot coming through the morningroom French window and there was Arthur, very hot and cheerful'; 'Said he wasn't coming in ... Stayed to watch us work ... as far as it was possible to work under the circumstances'; 'There was a loud halloo and there was Arthur'. Or he would be discovered on the road outside the loft or studio shouting up to Dora, 'talking to you is like eating a strawberry ice'. My mother would be leaning out of the window, and Arthur poking at his clay pipe, perhaps one which the charcoal burners down the lake had just seasoned for him.

He proposed to Dora more than once: 'I don't think he was serious. He seems to want to marry anyone and everyone – anything for a wife. I hope for his sake he doesn't really mean me'; 'He really is a dear in spite of his eccentricities. He is so nice and so utterly different from any man I know – indeed, he is the only man I know well ... better than I know my own brother but I don't want him to think I take more than a sisterly interest in him'. There appeared to be other candidates:

'I ignored everything he said and urged him to go to the other damsel and ask her. I wish he would make up his mind. I'm sure he would make a lot of money if he had some object to work for. As things are, he now thinks too much about himself . . . and he is much too young to retire into the country.' When they could keep off the subject of marriage, they had happy times together packing and unpacking Arthur's new teabasket 'of which he is immensely proud', or boiling up a kettle on a fire they had made together. 'We talked a lot of utter nonsense and I did enjoy it so much', Dora wrote. A plan for her to illustrate his first book did not come off, but she did a translation from the German for him for which he paid her £18 – 'An awful business'. Barbara helped him with the illustrations of his children's books. They remained on friendly and slightly flirtatious terms for the rest of their lives, and she continued to help him with illustrations.

When her parents could spare her, Dora took herself off to Paris. Unfortunately, while there she had a rare 'fit of utter inability to write letters', so we only have a very few tantalizing glimpses. As usual she was working very hard and, as usual, she was mostly anxious about what her father would say when she came back: 'I hope you don't expect to see marvellous works when I come home. I have a heap of life studies of various degrees of badness and about a hundredweight of short pose studies. I feel I have learnt a great deal, I'm only warning you not to expect too much.' She was trying to paint a portrait 'in a studio as big as a rabbit hutch, the model on the table set in front of the door – the only place for it – so that there had to be a rest every time anyone wanted to come in'.

My mother remembered this time when I was living in Paris in the 1930s, about twenty-five years later: 'Darling do try and keep your comb out of the butter', she wrote. And I was often to watch comb and butter edging inexorably towards each other, only managing to snatch them apart just in time!

But she did have some fun. At the Lent festival of Mi Carême she went to the masque ball with Hungarian friends dressed as pierrots in black dominoes – 'The feeling of skipping about without a skirt is most delightful'. They pranced down the Boulevard des Italiens which was ankle-deep in confetti, the air full of it, giving the atmosphere a faint, warm, dreamlike haze through which shone the streetlamps. 'There was a delightful feeling of spree in the air', but, to her surprise, the next day the boulevards looked as sedate as ever, only the gratings round the trees were full of little bits of coloured paper. She was careful to tell her parents that the pierrot costumes were homemade and only cost half a crown each and, what is more, the next morning she was at school by nine-thirty, none the worse. This was 1911.

In London, Barbara and Dora stood on chairs beside the Serpentine to watch a state funeral. 'The soldiers were lovely – simply slathers of them', said Dora, who had really hated leaving Paris. London had some compensations! 'Today I feel as if I was *getting on*. I did rather a good day's work at school ... I had quite a long lesson from Mr A. He gave me some awfully good advice and bestowed some rose madder on me, and some yellow ochre, and painted in a large piece of my background. He really isn't an idiot.'

In 1912, two years before she married Ernest and went off to Aleppo, Dora painted a large picture in oils of her father in his study. It might have been done by either of her parents – their styles are so similar. There is not a hint that she had ever seen paintings by Matisse or Gauguin or Picasso, who were exhibiting in Paris and had shocked the Academicians in London in 1911.

Photographs of Dora at this period show her as frail and willowy. She may have been consumptive – there are mentions of periods spent in sanatoriums and having to rest. Not much is made of this in letters. It was not thought proper in her day to talk about illness – or pregnancy. She had to ask my permission to tell friends when I was well advanced into expecting my first child in Jerusalem.

Just before leaving Paris, Dora had a card from Ernest saying he had gone to Aleppo and would probably have to stay there for a year.

Chapter Three

My two grandfathers, Assadour and Gershom, were not all that different from one another although they looked so different and had lead such different lives. They were both confident and happy men, sure of their standing in the world. When I try to imagine them now, I hear laughter and feel a sense of well-being. I can still see the front door at Lanehead wide open that night just after we had arrived from Aleppo. We were so excited about the snow that we escaped from our nurses and ran out naked onto the lawn. White Grandpa was the only one of the grown-ups who thought it funny and, I think, if Black Grandpa had been there, he would have laughed just as heartily. I remember White Grandpa's tears too when he had had a stroke and was telling me that he would never climb mountains again.

I was hardly three months old when I met my White Grandpa at Lanehead. I did not know my father then – he was away in France. Gershom's tall, blond good looks and charm must have won my infant heart. His fresh complexion and intense blue eyes were such a contrast to my father's lively Eastern face with the dark hair and eyes. My mother used to say that she had made up her mind to marry Ernest in the hope of having children with black curly hair like his. She was disappointed: none of us had curly hair! For me, this contrast in family types must have set up a dichotomy which confused my relationships for the rest of my life. I was the only one to inherit White Grandpa's bright complexion, blue eyes and decided chin.

At about a year old I was again staying at Lanehead. Gershom wrote:

Thankyou for the loan of the Poppet of all Poppets. Taqui is the darling of my heart ... she is a climbing girl. She swarms up the 'couloir' of my knees choosing hand-holds with deliberation and fearlessness. She climbs on me with a very tenacious grip. Tumbles don't aflict her. Perhaps she won't be easy to keep in a pen. She is a perfect wonder to me in her happy way of accepting the law even if she wants something else. That alone ought to make her a superwoman. She is curiously fond of pictures.

When they were both seventy, the two grandfathers were about equal in achievement. Black Grandpa had built himself a magnificent new house and, as it later turned out, was secretly thinking of getting married again. White Grandpa had published his great work, *Northumbrian Crosses in the Pre-Norman Age*. It was illustrated by hundreds of intricate pen-and-ink drawings of Christian and pre-Christian stones. His aim was to trace the evolution of the cross from two sticks poked into the ground as 'preaching posts' by the first missionaries, to the magnificent stone monuments put up all over Northumbria in the first millenium AD. Collecting the material had cost him much hard travelling, searching for stones sometimes hidden in buildings and hardly readable, and many hours with Indian ink and pen. In Aleppo, the Altounyan hospital had been busy with another sort of reconstruction – human limbs. Among Muslims death is preferred to amputation, which is seen as spoiling the body which God made. So my grandfather became clever at patching up, and even reconstructing limbs. An article in the *Lancet*, in 1927, says that the Altounyan Hospital in Aleppo had, to date, performed no fewer than 28,000 operations. Some of them plastic surgery.

If Black Grandpa had been allowed to visit the ancient churches of his ancestors in Eastern Turkey, the interlacing patterns on the tumbled stones might well have reminded him of pictures in White Grandpa's book. The dates of such cathedrals as Durham coincide with the last golden age of the Armenians in the first millenium AD. Our childhood magazine, 'The Aleppo Mercury', carried a serial by White Grandpa about an Armenian princess 'Taqui' who somehow managed to find her way to Northumbria! The story was set in that golden age. He must have known quite a lot about Early Christian Armenia.

The Altounyans and Collingwoods first became aware of each other after Ernest and Robin had become friends at Rugby. An invitation to Lanehead came quite soon and set the pattern for many years to come. Like Arthur Ransome, Ernest was very much in need of a home. He had to find an alternative to Belfast and Aleppo where he had spent all his holidays until then. The Collingwoods provided him with his first adventure just as the adolescent was trying to branch out on his own.

Later in life, in 1917, Ernest was to write his own account of his early years in his unpublished novel. He tells us that, 'having taken the daring step of marrying an Armenian in 1888 Harriet considered it her duty to bring up her son as a Perfect English Gentleman. At that time the British Empire was the most powerful in the world so the wisdom of her plan was obvious.'

My father first saw the light in a small flat in Paddington while Black Grandpa was in London taking the opportunity of a course in child medicine at St Mary's. Ernest was the only one of his family to have a British passport: 'His Britannic Majesty's Principal Secretary of State for Foreign Affairs requests and requires ... to allow the bearer to pass freely without let or hindrance ... afford such assistance and protection as may be necessary'. Impressive words for a little boy, and it was not surprising if he took them literally and if he was sometimes disappointed. When his younger sister, Norah, was being christened at a family gathering, he shocked everyone by cutting shrilly across his Irish uncle's sermon, 'If *she* has a new name I want one too. She can have *Hag* and I will be *John*'. He was careful to pronounce 'his Armenian name "Haïg" with naughty vindictiveness' because he knew it would annoy his mother. What was the use of the grand passport if he was saddled with this strange name? 'Altounyan' was bad enough.

Going to school in England was a dreadful shock for Ernest, but until that came he lived like a spoilt young prince. The world was planned for his enjoyment. Riding his white donkey about the streets of Aleppo, he would hear people whisper, 'There goes the son of the American'. 'Why on earth are we so famous?' he would ask his mother. In 'the exquisite security of a happy childhood' (as he described it in his novel), Ernest lorded it over his little sister, the household of servants and his white donkey. Though his mother and sister both seemed to think it very important to 'grow up good', there were so many much more important things to think about. His white donkey seemed to understand. Every afternoon when the sun had begun to lose its strength, at the evening call of the muezzin, Ernest sprang out of bed, where he had been whiling away the time of enforced siesta by scratching away still more of the plaster off the wall, and went down to saddle the donkey and to begin the daily competition with her. She never moved until she had been soundly thwacked, then she stepped soberly forward, swerving as she passed through the gate, just enough to scrape his leg, and she kept up a jog trot in case he had not quite recovered his stirrup. After this, treading on the paws of the sleeping dog was the only other amusement. At the top of the hill, rising in his stirrups, Ernest waved his whip over his head and brought it down on the donkey's rump with a tremendous roar, like a professional donkey boy. Jemima would fold back her ears and gallop. She wasted no time in admiring the view of the citadel but set to nibbling the fresh grass. Ernest unwisely dismounted although it would be hard to get on again without the groom holding the saddle. He would lie and watch his donkey nibbling. When the setting sun began to blaze back from the windows of the town, he usually managed to scramble into the saddle again. Jemima just gave him time to do this before starting on her headlong rush for home, through the evening strollers.

Although Aleppo was, on the whole, a safe place for a little boy to wander by himself, there were shadows, as Dora was to discover. One day, the old man who sat all day by their gate, acting as a sort of watchman, greeting callers and smoking his *nargile*, or hubble-bubble, did not come back from market. The tall Negress who ruled the kitchen, 'whose bare smooth flanks gave me my first lesson in tackling low', remarked that he was probably in prison. But he was soon back and the little boy realized that it was his father's word to the governor that had done it. So his father must be famous and strong. Perhaps stronger than God. He could answer his little sister's questions on God with confidence – 'It is quite simple you see, God (that is Our Heavenly Father) made me and you and everything. We must never forget Him . . . like the poor you know'. But: 'Did God make Mummy and Daddy?' 'I don't know.'

The life of the house depended on the Doctor's comings and goings. All day, the peal of the doorbell, the clang of the iron gate, the clatter of the horses' hoofs on the cobbles was the signal everyone waited for. The stable boy rushed out, the groom dismounted with his heavy bags of money and medical instruments, the Doctor was helped stiffly off his horse and there was the usual noise of the whip and stethoscope being thrown down on the hall table. Once he came home just in time to find both the children in tears. Ernest had been cruelly enticing a cat to play with a poor mouse he had caught in a trap. The game was amusing until the cat pounced and the mouse was reduced to a lifeless grey splodge. No fun at all. The Doctor turned the occasion into an anatomy lesson. Ernest cheered up and decided there and then to be a doctor.

It was round about the time of his ninth birthday that Ernest found himself being constantly reminded that he was a big boy now: 'Think of that'. On his birthday, a tall missionary who he called his godfather gave him a silver-topped walking stick which, at first, made him feel important and manly. He took it for a walk 'to where the houses were left behind and the road stretched between the harvested barley fields and bare stony tracts of red earth to the far blue mountains', where they went in the summer. But as the sun began to get too hot and hunger pangs began, the fun went out of it all. He no longer wanted to be grown up. Mercifully, when he got back, there was no one to see him hurl the stick to the top of the woodshed. Nine now. He could walk alone, but let that be a secret for a little longer. But that very evening, after he had gone to bed, 'the two linked figures on the terrace' decided he was to go to preparatory school in England – soon. At the cosiest time of the year, the carpets just spread on the stone floors and the woodburning stoves set up for the winter and roaring, he set out on a long journey across the sea. And at the end of his journey, 'School swallowed me up'.

So the 'Little Prince', the 'Pasha', the 'Famous son of the American' suddenly found himself in a topsy-turvy world where nothing seemed to make sense. He was immediately labelled 'Turkey' ('Where on earth was Armenia and what was an Armenian anyway?'). No use explaining that Turkey was nearer than India, where a lot of the boys' parents were; at least they hadn't got Armenian fathers. Were Armenians black? 'In this beastly place' it did not seem to make any difference trying to be good. If he worked, he was a 'swot' (whatever that was), if he was good at running he was accused of 'side' and 'sucking up' to masters. The little British gentlemen were worse than his enemies, the donkey boys, and he could not get away from them through the clanging iron gate. No use writing home any more: 'What was he doing here, he who had lived every moment of his life with servants, horses, and dust and sun that day after day poured onto the cream and white stone?'

The headmaster's report when he left for Rugby was sickening: 'a sterling plucky fellow whom we shall be sorry to lose. He takes the keenest interest in everything but in a clean manly manner. He has been a favourite of both masters and boys.' At Rugby he began to learn how to deal with 'virulent unpopularity' by studying another boy who 'facing foursquare to the world of school called himself a Jew before anyone else had time to think of it'. So Ernest called himself a 'mongrel' with tedious monotony all the rest of his life.

His holidays were spent on the long journey to Aleppo or on the slightly shorter journey to Belfast to stay with his uncle, Walter Riddall, who was his guardian. In Belfast he had to go to church too often and in Aleppo he became more and more unsure as to whether he would ever equal his phenomenal father. All his life he felt he lived in no man's land. This made him cling obsessively to people he found sympathetic or to places he felt were home. His reactions were never half-hearted and he expected other people to be the same: the whole world was either for or against him. So when Robin Collingwood invited Ernest to Lanehead in 1902, the magic worked for him at once. A strong feeling of 'coming home' wrapped him round and remained with him all his life. Apart from not having to go to church there were many things that were wonderfully different about the Collingwood way of life. The family of six (three girls and a boy and the parents) were all unlike anyone Ernest had ever met before. The special atmosphere of the house (the smell of oil paint the moment you were through the front door, the music before breakfast, the cheerful industry) was also new. Prob ably Ernest had never before heard so much serious talk about art. He may not have known who Ruskin was. Lanehead may have looked a little shabby compared to the affluent Victorian interiors at Antrim and Aleppo, but it looked like a palace to Ernest. The Collingwoods did not care to spend money on furniture unless it was special handmade furniture, and money was only important because it could leave you free to do what you wanted. From the moment he arrived, Ernest fell permanently in love with the house, its scenery and its inhabitants. He even quite liked rain when it was Coniston rain. In his unpublished novel he describes first seeing the beloved scenery through a 'bead curtain of rain drops'.

Robin and Ernest shared a bedroom. The rain often dripped through the skylight onto his bed. They only quarrelled when there was no wind for his daily sailing lessons. When at last he was able to take the boat out by himself, he immediately set out to Peel Island four miles down the lake. The novel, which does not seem to have had a title, was finished in 1917 – the year I was born and the year he was wounded out of the war at twenty-eight years of age. He describes his first sail alone to the 'sacred' island. Unless the wind was on the beam and he could make a long tack, it would take him four hours from the Lanehead boathouse. Sitting well on the gunwale, he skimmed close in along the wild stretches of the shore where the moor, free at last from all human habitation, swept down treeless to the coarse shingle. He felt a strange but very strong sympathy with it all. Battling against the cold spray, tacking and tacking across the lake, he forgot about the land where the sun always shone. He laughed loudly to himself in his crackling oilskins. The waves were black, when they were not purple, and their crests hit the boat like lead. With the brown sail reefed down to its limit, the boat bucked and quivered like a young horse. As he neared the island, he slacked off and drove straight at the slab where the water was deep, then up with the centreboard, down with the helm, gybe – two yards from disaster – a gentle crunch on the tiny beach as the mast and sailtop brushed the delicate branches of a tree. He tied up and jumped ashore ... the island was today 'completely his', as the novel said.

When he went to Cambridge, he found it more fun than Rugby. He ceased to be called a 'Turk', for one thing, and found people to appreciate his lively originality. One of them remembers him on a punting picnic, falling into the river in the middle of some witticism, and lying in the shallow water completely helpless with laughter. His friends were mostly literary. He spent his energies on everything except medicine. Very soon, disapproving eyes were upon him and worried letters sped East and West. His tutor wrote to his guardian that he 'was doing his medical work in a very casual way and reading more Browning and comparative religion than is good for him'. No one was surprised when a bad nervous breakdown forced him to return to Aleppo. 'He seems unable to settle down seriously.' Disraeli had been the same in youth, said Uncle Walter: 'It was considered in his case to be an inflammation of some covering of the brain'. The remedy, they thought, was travel and a complete rest from study. It was strongly hinted that perhaps he should travel to Aleppo and not come back. His uncle refused to take any more responsibility. He said so in a careful letter to his brother-in-law Theodore (the British version of Assadour). 'I do not suppose any serious mischief has manifested itself yet', he wrote, but he would be better off in Syria.

But Ernest flew like a homing pigeon back to Lanehead as soon as he could: 'I am staying with the Collingwoods, acquiring health and space every day. I badly needed something'. He needed release from the unbearably taut line stretched between Belfast and Aleppo on which he had been dancing like a puppet for so long. And, back in Cambridge, he was suddenly able to set to work with such a will that, very soon, he was house physician and then house surgeon at the Middlesex Hospital. He also won a prize for 'Psychology'. At

Cambridge he had got to know the Quaker John Rickman, one of the first students of the new psychoanalysis, who had been psychoanalysed by Freud himself. In their lifelong correspondence, my father always expressed his 'ambivalent feelings' about the new science ('psychological bilge', he would call it). But when in trouble, 'JR' was to be the person Ernest always turned to and, in spite of his avowed disapproval of 'taking too much notice of your confounded inner self', he was often pleased to extend a very grudging gratitude. It helped that JR was trained in medicine, was fond of earthy jokes and unable to resist food. He was very fond of my father, loyal to him through thick and thin. All of us regarded him as the best friend we had.

At Lanehead, Dora had hardly noticed Ernest, who was three years younger than herself, but the young things began to meet in London at a relaxed period when Dora had a clear conscience about staying because her treatment at the dentist went on and on. For once in her life she was allowing herself to 'mess about' – 'shake a loose leg', she called it: 'I am really doing disgracefully little work. I hope you don't want me back just yet'. She bought a new blue winter coat down to her ankles, costing a guinea. As they got to know each other, Ernest and Dora must have sensed a familiar atmosphere in each other's backgrounds which set them at ease and did not have to be written or spoken about. Each family was firmly bound together by a special skill which dominated their lives. With the Altounyans it was medicine, with the Collingwoods art. Often they went out with Arthur Ransome and Dora's sister, Barbara:

> I met Barbara and Ernest outside the theatre and we beguilded the hour and half very happily. . . . there were lots of interesting people there. Arnold Bennett looking quite as much like a grocer's assistant as he does in his portrait . . . the play was quite unlike anything that has been done before. Helena was beautiful. It was rather a shock to see Lillah McArthy with fair hair! The fairies were all gold all over and most strangely and outlandishly dressed. Puck was in scarlet with fuzzy fair hair, rather like Strewwelpeter and perfectly Pucklike . . . So wildly

unlike anything you would have expected. There were many calls for 'Barker' and after a long time Granville Barker and Cecil Sharp and the man who painted the scenery appeared. The audience would not go away till G.B. had made a speech . . . On Monday I hope to finish up my career of dissipation by having another tooth out and going to 'The Great Adventure'.

I imagine her 'career of dissipation' ended with her getting engaged to Ernest but family 'pebble' legend only relates that it happened in a non-corridor train (destination unknown). They were both looking after young sister Ursula's pug dog. Judging from Dora's letter to her mother at Lanehead, just after Ernest had been there to ask for her hand, you would imagine that she had only just noticed him: 'I'm glad you liked him and thought him nice . . . of course I know you liked him, long before I even knew him, so you did not treat him kindly on my account – but still – '. This was so typical of my mother's habitually cool, detached attitude, which strangers often mistakenly called 'cold'. From old habit, the rest of the letter is taken up with comments on an exhibition: 'your miniature and Pater's picture both lovely. Yours is the best we've seen . . . Pater's "Old Man" we liked very much too. . . . The show was as stodgy as ever'.

In 1914 war was declared. White Grandpa and Robin came to work in London. Barbara was in munitions for a time. Ernest was working at the Middlesex Hospital and, of course, worried about his father in Aleppo as Turkey took Germany's side. Dora wrote to Arthur Ransome on 6 September 1915, the day before her wedding:

> I'm going to be Married Tomorrow. You see we found that, after all, we could not bear to put it off for six months or a year, and September is a nice month to be married in. So it is going to be tomorrow. I'm 'dretfully' sorry you won't be there. You won't even know about it so you can drink our healths at the right moment . . . We are going to have a sort of studio place to live in I hope, the sort of place you would like, a big room with very little furniture and some big cushions to sit on the floor – just the place to tell Anancy stories in and Russian fairy tales. Ernest is

going to work at the Middlesex Hospital till next July as house surgeon. We shall come here as often as we can so the uprooting isn't *quite* so painful as it might have been. Anyhow I suppose it is silly to mind giving up a good thing in exchange for a better thing – and I shan't mind – much. I'm so glad you approve and think E. is 'quite all right'! You will really like him very much when you know him I know ... Your brother Geoffrey turned up on Saturday afternoon looking so well in khaki, walking from Finsthwait. He was very nice and jolly longing to go to France very soon. This is a scrappy letter but I can't write very coherently just now. Only wanted to send you a little scribble and my love. Beetle.

She enclosed a little sprig of bog myrtle or sweet gale as a reminder of their tea picnics. 'I hope it will still smell when you get it. I have fastened it in so the censor will not drop it out.'

On the 'very day', Ernest wrote to JR teasingly: 'I am as happy as when I was mad, but my happiness can be transmuted into work. If you could have looked inside me during the past month you would have chuckled and hailed me as an unacknowledged Quaker. I have no plans but trust to the will of God ... you need have no bother about getting married, you will be guided by your blooming inner light.'

Here again, the family 'pebbles' have been worn away with much handling: the facts of the wedding and honeymoon slip smoothly through the hand. Dora did not wear white but a Liberty silk dress printed over with roses and love-in-a-mist, which echoed the flowers in her bouquet. Ernest spent his last night as a bachelor at Brantwood with the Severns, Ruskin's friends and cousins. He was only with difficulty prevented from *sailing* across the lake to the wedding. The honeymoon was passed walking in the Langdales. Straight off from the 'breakfast', their knapsacks on their backs, they refused carriages offered. As Dora told the envious Arthur, 'we are going to walk off to Langdale and play about there for a bit.' In Hampstead 'they were still walking miles and miles, through sunset and twilight – just wandering'. Ernest played a lot of tennis and went skating on the ponds. In those days it was possible to carry a teapot onto the heath from home without the tea getting cold. It was a welcome respite from Aleppo. Turkey coming on the side of Germany meant that Aleppo, at that time in Turkey, was completely cut off. The odd letter or two fluttered in: 'I've heard at last from Turkey. The idiots are mobilising everybody from 20 to 45', Ernest told JR.

> Shops are being stripped and horses commandeered. My father has been appointed doctor to the military hospital for which he doesn't thank God. He lost four thousand pounds at the Deutsch Orient Bank. All hard earned cash, paid in sovereign by sovereign. But he has a little in his stocking, I believe. My uncle in Ireland has £150 for me so I am all right.

To the end of his life Ernest never faced the problem of money. Because his father kept the purse strings he never knew if he was fabulously rich or about to be bankrupt. When, at sixty-five, he received a cheque for £5 for royalties for his book of poems, it was the very first money he had earned independently of his father. Dora's letters hardly ever mention finance. It was almost as unmentionable as sex in those days but, considering her father-in-law was thought by Aleppo to be richer than Croesus, what she says in an early letter to her parents is surprising:

> You know that when I sent you that small cheque last spring I meant to send more in a few months. It seemed, at the time, that we could easily spare £5 a month, but since then I have had the very greatest difficulty in making ends meet, what with Brigit [the newest and last baby] and all the furnishings of the house. This month it is shoes for all the children, and winter clothes for them and the servants (and self if possible). E needs a decent hat and bang goes £2.

A cheque for ten shillings would, after all, have to do for both her parents' birthday presents. In one letter, Ernest threatens to 'liquidate this enormous show'; in the next, Black Grandpa has presented Dora with a necklace of real pearls for Christmas.

Eventually, in 1916, Ernest joined the Royal Army Medical

Corps and was soon busy doctoring sick blacks in London: 'He can't abide niggers but says they are very nice. He will write and tell me when The Push comes.' Poor Dora. A few weeks later, 'he is at last going to France. It is giving me such fits. He seems awfully pleased.' Ernest was never happier than when he was in uniform. It seemed to give him a new lease of life. While he was playing at being a captain, later a major and then a colonel in the RAMC, there was no possible doubt as to his identity or nationality. He felt he was accepted. 'E loves being under fire', wrote Dora to her parents in Lanehead as she was waiting for me to be born. He wrote from the Somme: 'The scenery is extraordinarily reminiscent of the lake on a dull day, while our barrage, spouting lines of white and brown, does noisy duty for a lake storm.'

I was born in Hampstead, 'looking very angry about something', as my aunt Barbara remarked. As the year was 1917, it was not surprising. The Russian Revolution could not have mattered much to me at the time, but the rejected Arthur Ransome, who was reporting for the *Manchester Guardian*, often wrote to Barbara from Moscow, describing what he could see from his hotel window, and it must have been talked about over my sloping head. The Great War had been going on for three years. In Aleppo my Black Grandpa was battling alone to keep his precious hospital intact and to do what he could to help the massacre victims flooding down from the north. What affected me most was the battle raging just across the Channel. My father was not present when I was born because he was busy there picking up the wounded in his ambulance – until he too became a casualty.

Having survived being buried alive by a shell, Ernest proudly wrote to his sister-in-law, Barbara: 'It is very amusing to think of what an absolutely conventional time I've been going through lately. I'm glad to go through it once, just to dispose of the whole business, and be able to speak with authority afterwards.' Ernest always volunteered for the most dangerous jobs, which amused his superiors, and they rewarded him. 'You're doing awfully well. I am extremely bucked with you', the ADMS was pleased to say. So, full of elation, Ernest tried to do even better. His ambulance went out again and again into the pitchy blackness, bringing back cases from 'the most torn up piece of earth imaginable'. Eventually, just before going home, 'I caught it, and here I am'. Dora was sent for at once. The kindly matron told her that there were 'a good many holes all over his body'. For the rest of his life his back was pitted with deep brown scars which horrified me when I saw him in a bathing suit, and we all knew, too, that there was a piece of German shell permanently in his kidney – it gave him pain from time to time – and there was that little finger, so characteristically deformed. He told us often how his life had been saved by a doctor who had noticed a foot sticking out of a heap of rubble. In spite of his bravado, and an MC, Ernest was glad, when all was said and done, that he did not have to 'face the racket' again.

Of course, I cannot remember that fateful afternoon in August when a policeman knocked on the door of 82 High Street, Hampstead with the news of my father's wounding. I was probably very angry indeed when, at three months, I found myself abandoned by my mother. In letters headed 'British Expeditionary Force in France', she said she had almost forgotten she 'had a baby over there', though she was knitting small socks and jackets for me as she sat by my father's bedside. I had certainly disappointed them by being a girl: I was to have been called 'Thorstein' after the Viking hero of my grandfather's novel. But they had to make do with 'Harriet', after my Irish grandmother, and 'Taqui', after the Armenian grandmother lost in Anatolia. But, boy or girl, far away in Aleppo, Black Grandpa shouted for joy when he got the news of my birth.

I was most carefully and lovingly looked after in magic Lanehead, my grandparents' home in the Lake District, but there has always been this nightmare of a large rubber object being thrust into my mouth. To his father-in-law, scribbling in pencil, Ernest wrote: 'It gives me such happiness to think that my child is being looked after by such wonderful people ... such a sense of beauty to think of the infant gurgling and sleeping and fattening among the untouched hills of the north.'

Just seventeen months later, another baby was born in Hampstead and named 'Susie' after her mother (call her Susan at your peril!). We girls all had Armenian names; hers was 'Arshalouis', meaning 'Dawn'. In 1919 my parents allowed themselves to hope for a new beginning. But poor little Susie looked at first like a 'famine baby', as my mother said. There was the flu epidemic and not very much for anyone to eat. But her large brown eyes and bright and sprightly expression made Susie 'fetching if not exactly pretty'. With my florid cheeks, blue eyes and curly red hair, I managed to look like a wax doll, although my expression remained sulky and angry.

The period when my father was back at home recovering from his wounds must have been a happy one for us all.

> It is really rather lovely to be in a state of perpetual leave only without having to count the days and minutes like so much gold. It makes quite a difference somehow to know that we shall be allowed now at last to be together for quite a long time for the first time in our lives. It is a dream come true.

Dora wrote to her mother while giving Susie her bottle, her paper supported on the baby's legs. On the blank spaces between the paragraphs are scribbles which I suspect are mine!

> I do want to get the babies to Coniston as soon as possible. Oh dear, I should like my children to be brought up at Lanehead. It seems such a little time since we were their age. I'm sure they would like the same things. Do you remember the long chains of rhododendron blossoms we used to thread one inside the other?

The Hampstead honeymoon did not go on for long. All too soon Ernest was better and 'Aleppo in hell' loomed.

Chapter Four

If ERNEST and Dora were tempted to dawdle about preparing to go out to Aleppo, they were soon hustled on by Black Grandpa, who was shopping in London for furniture and English clothes after attending the Paris conference where he had represented the Armenians of Western Asia. 'He is rather difficult to please. Must have the best of everything and is very decided about his taste. Heal's gave him rather a fit I'm afraid and we shall give him a lot more shocks in our choice of things', Dora wrote. But she was ready to let her smart sister-in-law, Norah, look over her clothes, 'Because of course she knows exactly what is wanted'. My mother's clothes were always picturesque, slightly Bloomsbury. They suited her 'Virginia Woolf looks' – her preoccupied, thoughtful expression, her hair looped up at the back and not a touch of make-up. French smartness was not her line. Lipstick was always barred. (My father used to declare he would 'cut us off without a shilling' if we used it.) A shiny nose was treated with a page of *papier poudré*. My mother never had her hair waved. But Aunt Norah daubed on the lipstick and everything else. I don't know what *her* father thought.

As Ernest and Dora prepared to leave for the East, there was much coming and going between Hampstead and Lanehead. Both grandpas were in London too. White Grandpa, staying with Dora, had been winding up his war work at the Admiralty. He wrote to Lanehead about 'the Armenian invasion' when Black Grandpa and Norah and an Armenian friend arrived suddenly from Paris:

They all turned up including another Armenian who could
not speak English. We have been scrimmaging, dragging
out more beds and blankets ... Norah asleep in a bed
beside Dora, Susie and the three men in the front room
variously disposed, I have a real folding camp bed in the
back room with a hearth rug for a mattress and my coat
and cloak to eke out the blankets.

I must have been at Lanehead!

The Collingwood grandparents never went out to Aleppo and
when Black Grandpa came to England he was either at
Lanehead or in a good hotel. This was a rare opportunity to get
to know one another better. Dorrie, waiting at Lanehead, would
be glad but not surprised, wrote White Grandpa, to hear that
'Dr Altounyan is as nice as ever and even more so. I am very
fond of him. Norah is also very nice and I don't see that she is
spoilt at all. Dora gets on perfectly well with them.' Of course,
they were all worried about the Armenians, and White
Grandpa wrote that he hoped their business would be much
advanced by Black Grandpa's presence in Paris: 'I do hope and
pray that all the dear people will escape without a scratch'. He had
just read in the paper, he told his wife, that Turkey wanted peace.
'No doubt it is too soon to rub one's hands but it is reported that
Turkish negotiators are on the way to Aleppo'. It was 1919 and the
future of Syria or any part of the East was still uncertain.

One last visit to Lanehead and the November day came
when they would have to leave. Dora kept a diary of the
journey. 'The sunrise on the mountains and the lake with mist
floating on it' was 'too much of a good thing' for her – it made
her want to weep. We started out – Ernest, Dora, Susie and
myself – much too early in the huge hire car and got to
Ulverston Station long before it was open. I was sick even
before Greenodd. But the station master was an old friend. He
and his wife went down in family history for the way they
welcomed us at that early hour. We had bread and butter in
front of a huge coal fire (the last we were to see for many a
long year). Over the mantelpiece was a picture by Dora's
mother. But once we had left the safety of Ulverston things did
not go so well. The train ('Preston Crew and London only –

non-stop') kept breaking down, seven times in all: 'the engine had a leak and could not get steam up. The water kept pouring out as fast as it was put in.' Matters were not helped by passengers wandering up and down the line giving advice. Ernest and Dora were thankful to reach Euston 'within the day'. In the hotel, my mother found the most comfortable bed she had ever slept in. All the family had breakfast in it the next morning to recover.

What with one thing and another, the journey to Aleppo took a month and two days. My mother was nearly thirty-three and I two and a half. I think we were closer then than we were the rest of our lives. We were both so excited at the new world we were seeing from the trains and boats which were our home for so many weeks. According to her, I seemed to notice and appreciate everything. The relieved surprise with which she keeps on commenting on my extreme goodness makes me think that I was probably going through the 'terrible two' stage at the time: 'cheerful and very good'; 'wonderfully good'; 'most awfully good'.

Both my mother and I, at times, suffered from homesickness. I was for ever chattering about what I had done with my grandparents and aunts left behind at Lanehead. After all, I had seen a great deal of them while my parents were busy getting ready. 'Oh! Hampstead!' exclaims Dora passionately in a letter otherwise full of practical details (How much in her post-office savings account? Library books to go back? Birthday presents to be bought? The aluminium double-boiler which Barbara wants).

> I do wish you were still at No. 82. It makes me quite weak to think of it. I'm glad, in a way, that no one is living there. I don't mind upstairs so much . . . Oh Hampstead . . . someday when we are elderly and rich we are going to buy a house there (82, including both parts) and settle down surrounded by our numerous children and grand-children – and, of course, we shall have a house in the Lakes too.

When we got to an old-fashioned solid-looking hotel in Beirut (the old Bassouls where all the family used to stay in the old days), I said at once that it was 'just like Gwanny's Wanehead'.

It was the first substantial building I had found myself in during several weeks of boats and trains.

As we sped through France on our way to Marseilles, my parents noticed a good many traces of bombardment. 'E. said there were trenches but it was too dark to see them. Some of the carriages had double eagles on them and notices in German,' wrote Dora. Like Cézanne discovering the South of France in middle age, Dora was dazzled by colour and light and the sheer strangeness of everything:

> I saw the first olives I have ever seen, and oleanders and vines, and the quaintest little towns, with large crinkly tiles on the roofs. There were queer limestone rocks and unfamiliar trees and buildings. It got more exciting as we neared Marseilles. It is a mixture of Italy and Africa [neither countries had Dora been to]. The people are already 'Eastern looking' ... We have never eaten so many grapes in our lives before.

Not even, I should imagine, in Mr Ruskin's hothouses at Brantwood, where my mother had last seen such luxury.

Very soon, they were, as she said, 'ploughing through the Mediterranean. I had heard it was blue but I had not expected this glorified washing blue – even when the sky is grey [unlike Coniston Lake on sulky days].' My parents got to know a lot of people, some of them at *too* close quarters:

> Officers' wives of the aggressive Anglo–India type [it was a P. & O. ship going to India] – most unattractive ladies ... The women seem to get it worse than the men, and they are bad enough – for instance, a great fat brute with a face which makes one pity the people he governs. His wife's eyes were like a snake's.

Luckily there was also a couple from Windermere ('very nice' – naturally!). Ernest spent a lot of time talking to a 'little old black bearded Russian' who turned out to be a very distinguished Zionist – one Chaim Weizmann.

All the time, Ernest was 'a marvel ... ready to do anything, even bath and dress Taqui'. But in Alexandria it was *he* who was overcome by the heat – and perhaps by meeting 'The East' yet once more. But Dora could not be kept on board the ship; venturing ashore by herself, she fainted. When she came round, about five men were spraying her face with eau-de-Cologne, holding smelling salts to her nose, rubbing her hands . . . They sent her home in a cab and 'didn't even pinch the two five-pound notes I had in my bag'. Dora always had to be really ill before she would 'waste time' in bed. She scorned the way some of the Aleppo ladies complained constantly that they were *fatiguée*. But in a postscript heavily marked 'CONFIDENTIAL', for her mother she tells her to expect a grand*son* in May and admits that she has been feeling 'mouldy' since we set out.

In Alexandria, we drove through gardens 'smelling like everything in paradise' and saw plants and trees which only grew in the grandest conservatories at Brantwood. Dora saw fresh dates growing on the trees and, 'do you know, they are bright scarlet'. The 'native' quarters they drove through were 'incredibly primitive and genuine looking'. But they did not like Port Said at all:

> Port Said is a loathly place. Saturday afternoon was spent in coaling. All portholes were shut and coal was brought on board by hundreds of coal black demons in coal black rags running up and down a plank from a barge with baskets on their backs and all yelling all the time. The air was full of coal dust and there was nothing to do but go below and take off most of one's clothes and lie and perspire. It was impossible to sleep for, besides coaling, there was also loading and unloading going on and the cranes rattling.

Changing from the British P. & O. liner to an Italian boat at Alexandria took them another stop further from home. Italians were nice but, on the whole, you could not trust them far. Had not they just escaped being swindled out of their state cabin? 'Not nearly so clean . . . cockroaches in the cabins, quite small brown ones, and no doubt harmless, but still . . . There were also – not fleas – but something much nastier – bed bugs.'

Though she had been interested in Egypt, Dora was keeping her real feelings for Palestine. She had found the beginnings of

The Unknown Remembered Gate

the Suez Canal, seen from a native *kaik*, interesting but 'rather horrible' – I suppose because the country was so featureless, meaning flat: no mountains. Now, in spite of the cockroaches in the new ship:

> The great moment came when I was pinning up my hair and looked out to see the coast of Palestine. In a few minutes we slowed down and anchored off Jaffa. Alexandria is all very well, with its English and French shops and harbour and everything civilised – but when you get to Jaffa it is all quite different. Here really *is* the East. There is no harbour of any sort and cargo which has to be taken aboard comes out in large rowing-boats. Dozens of little boats come out rowed by Syrians in short extremely wide trousers.

She was pleased to be able to recognize mountains – Mount Carmel, for example – from her memory of old Bible maps. 'Then, sure enough, when we got round the headland, there was the flat land (coloured yellow on our map) where the mountains recede from the sea. So exciting to see things that one has known all one's life.'

But they were not 'home' yet. They had hoped to travel to Alexandretta in their Italian boat but the town was still under French occupation'. The trouble with disembarking and taking the train at Beirut was an epidemic of cholera raging there. But Ernest made a fuss and they were smuggled off the boat in spite of quarantine orders.

The next 'joke' was a train strike: 'just like in England'. Luckily, the British were 'in occupation'. Ernest, as a very recent RAMC, had plenty of leverage with the army running the trains. The quarantine regulations did not seem to be too strict. 'When we were in the train a man suddenly reached in at the window and began feeling my pulse. I was astonished, but of course it was a medical examination in case of there being any cases of plague on board.' They brought a whole bough of oranges, several water melons, and an earthenware jug of water for the journey, also a bottle of ammonia to dab on their insect bites. The journey was hot except for when the train toiled over the high Lebanon where they saw scenery 'like Wetherlam.

Blackberries and autumn crocuses'. But very soon they were down in the plain again. At Rayyak, in those days a most desolate spot, there were again cockroaches in the soup, and bedbugs, 'but we were lucky to get a bed here in the British military hospital where people were delighted to meet a family straight from England. We slept fairly well in spite of goods trains playing about under our windows all night.'

It was dark when they at last saw the lights of Aleppo the next night. Saïd, the groom, who knew Ernest from boyhood, was on the platform. 'It is cooler here – a little', wrote Dora. First thing the next morning she was drawing a plan of the house: 'We have a beautiful room opening onto a terrace covered in vines.' Arriving at midnight, they had found themselves in a cool, quiet hall with a huge table in the middle and a sofa against each wall. 'Floor, walls and table *and* sofas are all covered with carpets, of course, also three of the six doors have carpets hung in front of them.' (Black Grandpa collected carpets. I used to hide in one dark room which was full from floor to ceiling with them, wrapped in white sheets, like corpses, I thought. The windows being kept permanently closed, the smell of mothballs was overpowering.) Ernest had his thirtieth birthday a few days after they arrived, 'and he feels very old'. Ernest and Dora explored the souks 'the most wonderful places. Miles of narrow streets roofed, some with stone vaulting, some with mere boards and trellises with vines ... on each side little shops which are just holes like railway arches only smaller. In front of each there is a raised platform on which you can sit to bargain – and sip Turkish coffee.' They had come to buy household pots and pans. It would be at least six months before the things from Heal's arrived. This must have been one of the very few times in their lives in Aleppo that Ernest and Dora wandered through the 'bazaars' as they called them, unselfconsciously, as if they were still in Hampstead. It was not 'the thing' to be seen wandering about on foot. (Too poor to own a car?) Also Ernest complained because too many people tried to have 'free consultations'. Queues formed if they stopped. The doctors usually sped about in their cars or left them waiting at the entrance to narrow alleys. If we wanted to go into the souks we were usually accompanied. To be seen carrying parcels or heavy baskets was also a sign of poverty. But Dora

> longed to wander invisibly, and penetrate into the doors and passages and courtyards and strange windowless streets and see what really happens there. When one forgets there is such a thing as sanitation, there is something that catches hold of one. Though I am not one of those who delight to live the native life in native houses among native 'queetures' [baby talk] and other minor horrors of the East.

Dora does not often mention the hospital in her letters, probably because she spent so much time keeping it out of their lives, but in that first letter she wrote: 'The hospital is a jolly place paved with red and grey marble. It is the most marvellous place you ever saw. I must write you a whole letter about it some day.' She never did. 'E. is fearfully busy while his father is still away and is much annoyed because his patients keep "dying on him" so to speak. He has several very bad cases, but I think he is quite enjoying himself really.' This rather strange remark of my mother's might have puzzled her parents but they probably knew Ernest well enough to guess what Dora meant. Ernest was nothing if not enthusiastic about everything he did – even tending dying patients! As for Dora:

> I am trying to fill the part of mistress of this house with dignity and severity tempered with indulgence – no light job I can tell you when it has to be done with such a defective vocabulary as mine. Broken language and dumb show do not inspire respect.

She had to take over the running of the house as soon as she arrived because her sister-in-law Norah was away on business involving Armenian refugees. She herself was to become involved in 'relief work' very soon. But until she could speak, as she said, it was really 'nothing but a farce'.

> This morning I had to dispense charity to a woman sent on by somebody else (just as tramps do at home) wanting to get back to her home in Beirut. She spoke Arabic, so

> Habib [the cook] had to translate into Turkish to someone who could speak Turkish and English in order to translate it to me. So, after much consultation, I gave her some money and had my hand kissed. I am longing to be able to talk. I am working hard on Armenian but that will only enable me to talk to about a quarter of the people I meet. ... I am picking up a few words though whether Armenian Arabic or Turkish it is difficult to know. I have had my first lesson in Armenian from a woman who speaks a little German. The servants speak all three languages. Armenian is rather uncouth though it does not sound bad when spoken. There is absolutely nothing to hang on to, or recognise, as anything one has met before – except an occasional word like Latin, for it is an Indo-Germanic language after all – though a rather distant relation.

My mother's hobby was languages, so she enjoyed the variety. She even began to learn Japanese. She was passionate about accents, worried that we would learn to speak French the drawling Lebanese way. As for the Americans: 'I can't think how really refined people like them can speak so'.

> Life is full of interest in these parts and if the highlights are not lighter the shadows are certainly much blacker than anywhere else I know. Only I don't consider it an ideal place in which to bring up a family which is my one aim in life at present. If it weren't for the family I would love it and as it is I do like it very much. Taqui likes it too.

In those first days when we were getting used to the 'strange ways and things and people' together, neither of us being able to speak, my mother and I were both onlookers.

Dora saw very little of Ernest. 'The men go off to hospital (on the other side of the town) after breakfast and when they come back I am always too sleepy to do anything but go to bed.' My mother was always 'a lark', best in the early morning. She never could get used to the Oriental way of staying up very late. She could not keep her eyes open at a late dinner party – just when Ernest was beginning to relax after a hard day and was anxious to talk. That winter, so many people were ill that the two doctors never had any time to themselves.

That first Christmas would have been extremely jolly but for the fact that Norah was ill:

> She is *very* ill and doesn't seem able to get better. They seem to think it is a particularly bad form of malaria and perhaps influenza too. Anyhow she has a high fever most of the time and headache and sickness . . . On Christmas day she was so ill that she could hardly speak . . . So of course we cannot have anything in the way of a Christmas festivity.

But, for Dora, the first Christmas in her new home could not help being like an iridescent bubble floating precariously against a dark background. It was 1919. Half the world in ruins. Aleppo clogged with the victims from the deportations huddled miserably in the winter's cold. Outside the glow of the huge Christmas tree in our drawing-room, outside our house, was darkness and desolation. But: 'We still had a very nice time and it was great fun'. Even though it was 'pouring wet and dark like it might have been in England'. With the help of the servants she made garlands of ivy and hung them round the hall. The tree had been ordered from a wood fifty miles away in mountains which were soon to be permanently over the new border in Turkey. Three small trees arrived on the back of a very small donkey, but that would not do. Ernest scoured Aleppo on horseback and found a better one. In the cellar they found an 'immemorial' box of decorations, which perhaps came from Ireland, in my grandmother Harriet's time, 'rather dilapidated but enough to make a nice bright tree'. The new silver from England was brought out for the first time, and polished by Ernest. Brass and copper dishes were piled high with oranges. Brass candlesticks and dark, shining lemon leaves were arranged down the centre of the table. The servants had never seen a 'proper Christmas' before, nor had the many visitors who kept on dropping in to pay polite calls. 'No one had time to talk Turkish to gentlemen in tarbushes. I hope they managed to amuse each other with coffee and sugared almonds.' For Dora, there were a crimson and gold *mashlah* (an

Arab cloak) and diamonds in an oriental shape from Ernest, and a ring with a ruby in it from her father-in-law. After supper, she sat in the drawing-room eating sweets languidly: 'I haven't seen so many for years: crystallized apricots, and Turkish delight and some real English chocolate'. For me, it was the first Christmas I would remember. I 'ate an orange with perfect neatness and propriety.'

She was really the chief feature, so to speak, of the party, in her little blue muslin dress, giving out packets of chocolate and kisses to anyone who wanted them – servants and all! I hardly looked at anything else the whole time, she was so sweet and good and happy. 'Nice being Christmas for a change', I said, as I was carried off to bed at last.

But when it was all over, I was frightfully naughty, smearing myself all over with permanganate of potash when my mother wasn't looking, 'so she can't have cake today'. 'I've left my White Grandpa at Lanehead,' I kept on saying, 'but he will come to Aleppo one day.' When our furniture at last arrived and the little chair I had last seen in Hampstead suddenly appeared over the brow of the hill on top of a cart, I thought he really had come. And on New Year's Day, Dora wrote: 'I do so much want to see you and have all the old things and times back again'. The parcel meant for Christmas was two months late and arrived in a hopelessly battered condition. 'I loved the rosemary, which still smells sweet, and the little shrivelled spray of jasmine and the bay leaves.'

Chapter Five

NINETEEN-NINETEEN was an itchy, uncomfortable and dangerous time for everyone all over the Western world. When we arrived in Aleppo we did not know what the name of the country was going to be. Syria had been part of the Ottoman Empire for four hundred years. My parents hoped that the British Army would stay for ever – 'Long may the British Army occupy Syria'. But hardly had we arrived when we could see the Army tents opposite our house being struck and, very soon, the last of the British were marching away. 'We feel rather orphaned without them', said my mother. She tried hard to make sense of the situation in letters to her father. 'The air is thick with rumours.' There were stories of fighting between the French and the Arabs on the railway line, and of the English coming to retake the town ('absurd of course'). Bad trouble between the English and the Arabs, fighting between the English and the Turks – hard to make sense of.

Pages and pages of my mother's letters were taken up with a description of how King Faisal visited our hospital and an Arab flag flew over the building where no sort of flag had ever flown before. The English matron carefully placed a small Union Jack where the King could see it. A few weeks later, the same King was being chased out of Syria by the French. And now Aleppo was welcoming the French. They did not look very different to the English, to my mother and me, looking out of the window. There seemed an endless succession of reviews to welcome conquering generals, French or English or Arab, and then demonstrations of protest against them from the citizens of Aleppo. I remember a most satisfying explosion just after the

French marched in. There was a clap of thunder and a huge cloud of smoke above the gardens to the west of Aleppo – not too near, but I could see bricks flying up. The Turks had used one of the mosques as an ammunition dump and it had been blown up by mistake by a cigarette falling on a shell.

Then there was the ceremony at 'The Monument', a sort of Cleopatra's needle, some miles out of Aleppo, set up to mark the spot where some British had fallen in the last battle with the Turks before things were sorted out. When they first came in the French had tried to pretend – or so it seemed to my parents – that they had been the heroes of this battle, though the names of the British fallen were carved on the monument for all to read. But when it no longer mattered, by the time I was allowed to go to the ceremony (when I was considered old enough to behave properly): 'This time it was tastefully decorated with flowers and wreaths and Union Jacks and not a single French flag in sight. Nobody could be better at majestic tact than the French when they have a mind. The general planted himself in front of the monument and took off his kepi and there was a two minutes' silence. Then, if you please, the military band struck up God Save the King – no Marseillaise or tricolour or anything. It was most touching', wrote my mother. But I remember how shocked she was when we did not realize that it *was* 'God Save the King'. Perhaps that is what decided her to send us to boarding school as soon as we were old enough. Consuls to be observed at reviews gave us constant amusement. Like the rest of Aleppo, we formed our opinion of any country according to the person who happened to be representing it at Aleppo. But feathers and gold braid never deceived my mother: 'He is not out of the top drawer. He looks like a grocer's assistant and his wife a bar maid'. When that was her verdict, I knew that there would not be many dinners and invitations between the households – just politeness. The golden age of Consuls was in the early thirties, just before we were sent to school. Doing the *Times* crossword in twenty minutes was, we gathered, a sign of brilliance. But a lot could be forgiven if people liked sailing or knew the Lake District. There were so few 'English' (as we called them) who came to Aleppo in those days that we really had to make the best of them, and forgive a dropped 'h' or two.

The Unknown Remembered Gate

The great festival for us was the King's birthday. One year, I remember my mother sent us along with sixteen precious raspberries (she must have grown them herself on the terrace) in a basket. We thought we were meeting the King himself, or at least someone who knew him very well. When the fat Proconsul placed his hand on our dark, silken heads and said, 'we are proud of our subjects', we did not think of giggling.

The Union Française or French Club was where my parents went occasionally for 'a taste of what they call high life'. Most of the foreigners and upper-class Syrians belonged. About fifty families (Syrians, French, army, diplomats, missionaries, businessmen) formed the social circle. The yearly fancy-dress dances happened at Mi-Carême. For months beforehand, costumes were worked on in a fever of excitement. When Ernest went dressed as an Egyptian mummy, 'he looked a terrifying sight with gilded sticking plaster over his moustache and eyebrows. Hardly anyone recognized him'. Dora was 'a Greek dancer out of a Bakst ballet, in a wig made of twisted rope painted with gold'. Another year, Ernest was a harlequin in tights, again painted by Dora, and then, most daringly of all, as Nijinsky in *Après-midi d'un faune*. One year, the black king and queen got first prize. Dora very much enjoyed making the costumes and was pleased that, 'even at forty', Ernest had such good legs. But the dancing wasn't really her scene: 'we watched the various local variations of the Charleston and the tango and even had a go ourselves, though I must say that leg waggle looks just like a wound up mechanical doll and very difficult to learn'. As time went on, she was frightfully bored at going to these dances and cursed all the time she was making the wretched costumes. 'People only dance with me because of politeness and I wish they would not.' And she came to hate dancing more and more. She dreaded it as a sign of the onset of my father's manic fits.

In the six months from November to May after we had arrived, I successfully ignored my mother's swelling front and the giggling hints of the servants in languages I could only dimly understand. So I was terrified to wake up one night to find my parents apparently leaving again. I don't know how they calmed me. Mavis Araxi, born in 1920, turned out to be a most satisfactory baby, after my mother had got over the disappointment of her being a girl. She managed to feed her for much longer than her first two babies, due, no doubt, to the good food and sunshine after wartime Hampstead. I asked if she had any legs.

When I was recovering from smallpox which had afflicted me, my father said, because I had not been properly vaccinated while he was away, my mother was still feeding Susie and had to change her clothes completely each time she went back and forth through the curtain soaked in carbolic which hung between me and the outside world. I remember her cutting out strings of paper camels for me which swung their way across my feverish dreams. When alone, I lay and watched the shadows of things moving in the street which the brilliant sunshine cast on the ceiling. There were noises, too, to tell me of the outside world, such as the sound of milk squirting into a can when the scraggy cow stopped at our gate to be milked. When my window was open, there would be the strong smell of horses from the stables below and the noise of their hoofs on the cobbles. My hands had to be tied all the time so that I did not scratch, but this meant that I escaped with no scars which everyone said was a miracle.

As I recovered, it was still the horses which frightened and fascinated me. They were so large and there was always the danger of being lifted high on to someone's saddle. Everyone except my mother was always on horseback in those days. She was as nervous of them as I was. My father's frisky black horse and the talk I overheard of shells bursting on the Somme combined in one of my collection of recurring nightmares. Sometimes I woke to hear his angry shouts at the animals in the stables below us, fighting in the night. In spite of my timidity, the first attachments I formed, at the age of about three, had to be to animals. They were more my size, and controllable. I sympathized with the dogs who were beaten by the servants for making puddles. I learned about birth from watching chickens pecking their way out of eggs. I envied the pigeons who deigned to come down and take grain from my fat little hands. The wild

The Unknown Remembered Gate

ones made their perilous nests from a very few sticks on the very edge of our windowsills. They were brave! Their cooing we heard all day, like the wind which moaned against our faded green shutters. But they seemed so much less friendly than the birds and squirrels hopping about the lawns in Granny's Lanehead. And there was no dust there. In Aleppo it was nearly always dusty with a wind which ruffled our clothes, flattened our hair against our faces and kept the dust whirling about in the streets.

When, at last, I was allowed to get out of bed, I found that outside the bedroom was a terrace covered by a vine trellis. The wall was low and so wide that I could lie safely and comfortably on it and watch the Jewish school next door. How I envied all those little girls, dressed in black overalls, crammed together on hard wooden benches forever chanting. I saw them hold out their palms to be hit with a ruler. But I wanted to be friends with them, to walk to school every morning with my satchel on my back. We were never allowed to buy things in the streets, never allowed to taste the brilliant skeins of spun sugar heaped on straw trays, carried on the heads of debonaire youths. We were forbidden the scarlet toffee-apples which looked so inviting – no doubt they were coated with flies and dust – but sucking the handle of my skipping rope was a very poor substitute!

I first learned about death when my pet rabbit died and one day I was certain that I was about to die myself. Our breakfast room was warmed with a great brass *mangal* full of red coals. One day, I tripped on the carpet and fell with my arm across the fire. I was certain that I would be burnt up at once. I remember screaming, 'I don't want to die, I don't want to die.' One of my names was Harriet. My mother had often read me the story of 'Harriet and the Matches'. My father wrapped my poor arm in pink lint. It all stuck. For weeks there were daily journeys across the town to the hospital and sharp little scissors cutting round the scabs. I'm sure I did a lot more shrieking, but slowly I realized that I was not going to die – this time.

Two years after the birth of Mavis, 'The Little Prince' (as the purring ladies of Aleppo called him) was born on 24 October 1922, and I expect Dora could hardly believe she had a boy at last. 'For various complicated reasons', he was called Roger Edward Collingwood. 'Roger' after the hero of Ernest's unpublished novel (by this time White Grandpa's novel *Thorstein of the Mere* seems to have been forgotten). 'Edward was probably a gesture of friendship towards Ernest's French brother-in-law with whom he always had an ambivalent relationship. Bright eyes peeped at us out of the folds of my mother's long cloak as she carried him home to us from the hospital. That mischievous but somehow benevolent sparkle was there even then. In the group photograph we had taken for our first journey back to England the year after he was born, he is just a bundled shawl revealing a quiff of hair and those eyes. Of course, he was always a tease – it was an Altounyan habit.

Like my father, Roger hated to see anyone sitting quietly. 'Anything wrong?' he would say. We got used to those sudden shrieks in the ear, book knocked over, as he brushed past on his swooping scooter, perhaps even then practising low night flying. Once, and perhaps more than once, we girls had to wrap him in the nearest rug, beating him with broom handles. That imitation of cleft-palate talk, perfected as a boy, usually began telephone conversations – impossible to reproduce the sound in print! He fancied himself doing imitations, his conversation was full of 'cameos' of people he had met and thought amusing. He was hardly ever still or quiet. I remember him in his top bunk on a sea journey, annoying us with a bombardment of tiny planes – with propellers – fashioned out of matchsticks. If only we had known that he was inventing the spinhaler! But he was all my mother wanted and imagined in a son:

> I am making him some little tussor smocks for the hot weather in which he looks a perfect angel. He walks about a lot now and really I think gets more entrancing every day. Such a lot of words he knows and still talks his own language like a little bird singing.

Like the rest of us he spent a lot of his first winters being ill. Dora and Ernest had sleepless nights nursing him – never mind the hospital full of nurses just over the road.

> We've had a pretty nasty time with him. Only one lung is infected ... the little boy looks prettier than ever sitting among his pillows. His little nose stands up like a rock out of his face which has got rather thin. His eyes and long lashes are blacker than ever and his little mouth more delicately cut. It is a blessing he has not got curly hair.

In the next letter he is 'swallowing quinine pills without water and enjoying it'. My father used to give us 'pill drill' lobbing pellets of bread down our throats to practise for the inevitable seasons of illness.

Almost before he could walk Roger was showing signs of his passion for people in the mass, staggering into the nurses' dining-room, hanging on to the door handle shouting 'Hullo'. Like all babies, he loved 'helping': 'You should see him carrying stones', working away like a little beaver. My father spent part of a summer holiday building a tennis court: 'Today I discovered the seat of his pants hanging like rags from his little behind. He had been sliding down some rocks. He is such a joy'; 'Yesterday I heard a fearful noise going on in the children's room. Roger beating Susie and calling her a 'horrid horrid girl'. Susie was doing the teasing this time – calling him 'a baby'.

It was a good thing Roger had inherited his grandfather Assadour's equable character (as Aleppo noted with relief – nothing artistic or bookish about him) because he had his share of trials. From a very early age his knees and wrists were swathed in bandages because of his chronic eczema. Many a Sunday my mother would have to spend much time sewing them onto him because the nurse we had at the time was of a particularly strict Christian Church which forbayed her to lift a needle on the sabbath.

After the triumphant birth of a son and heir, Dora and Ernest had no more children till 1926 when Brigit Mary Lucine was born. Another girl. 'We could have done with a spare', was Ernest's comment. The poor child was born in the heat of summer with an alarmingly high temperature because she had malaria. Because she was so much younger than the rest of us, Brigit was almost an only child. When she was still small, we were removed to boarding school in England. When the rest of us were doing war work, Brigit was still having to go to school – in Jerusalem. We moved to the new house in Aleppo the year she was born.

Breakfast time was the only meal when we were all together as a family. My father was still in his clinic at lunch time and, until we went to school, our last meal of the day was a sort of nursery tea from which my mother took care to be absent. We behaved rowdily. Our father had a lot of spare energy at breakfast time. He always went riding before work. He liked to treat us as if he was drilling a squad of soldiers. 'Sit up straight. Have you brushed your teeth?' he would bark, with one finger on the bell to the kitchen to order his cheese and egg – his favourite food. Servants went scurrying in every direction. My mother, as usual, tried to calm him. Sometimes a patient who had been waiting in the hall since dawn saw his chance and tried to put his head round the door – and was noisily repulsed. There was always trouble if the horses were not where ordered, or the driver, whose job it was to wind the kitchen clock, set it one minute fast or slow.

Called 'the tribe' by the English grown-ups, we spent all day together and usually shared bedrooms. We eldest girls even had a collective name: Taqsuzitty. We had lessons round a big table all together, even in the days when we had a governess and were all at different stages. In the afternoons we usually went out in the car: in the short spring to pick flowers which were wonderful in those days: tulips, anemonies, irises and all sorts of wonderful things growing in the standing corn – and no rules against picking them. Sometimes my father arranged educational trips into the souks to watch copper pots being hammered out or wooden stools being made. We had few friends although I'm sure our parents made efforts. I remember a birthday party when I was quite young, at which I was unable to talk to any of the children officially invited. No wonder I longed to go to school.

Because we were physically always together and very near to each other in age, I got to think that we thought the same. I have discovered that this was by no means so. Like seedlings which have not been 'potted on' soon enough, we had not enough room to grow. It took me a long time to begin to discover who I really was. When my own children were small, I watched with amazement and admiration as they made their own friends, going off to school from the age of five with an independence I was never allowed.

People say, 'you must have had a wonderful childhood' – and it was wonderful. We lived in Syria to a standard only the very rich can do in England today. But I longed for friends.

I can't remember how I learnt Armenian or when there began to be a difference between the five languages I heard round me. Quite soon I could say *'shnorhagalliem'* to my Black Grandpa when he put sugar on my porridge. But we usually talked English to him and to our parents. I must have learnt *'voch voch'* early – meaning 'no' in Armenian. Those huge women in wooden clogs and aprons seemed to be free to barge into any room I happened to be in. They were always picking me up, pinching my cheeks, hugging me, shouting words at me as if I could understand better that way. There was always so much noise. Till I was three I had probably not heard anyone shouting and now there were loud voices in the streets, all the time, which quite drowned out the cars in those days when it was all voices and the clip-clop of horses' hoofs on cobbles. Gradually I learned to sort out the voices – English, French, Arabic, Armenian and Turkish.

One had to try and keep them in compartments. In a confusing world this was desperately necessary. If my mother tried to talk to me in Armenian, I looked shy: 'Baby too ickle to say dat'. As I grew up, I understood that most of the people in the house – except my mother – were either Armenian or partly so. But my father never spoke the language. He refused to. And a lot of the servants seemed to know Turkish better. But I soon found out that Turks were the enemy. Our nurses told me about them – when they thought my parents were not listening. Something horrible had happened, not so long ago, and not so far away either. But we were told that Aleppo was an Arab town. A lot of the patients in the hospital were Arabs and our manservant, Saïd, spoke the language too, and did accounts in

Arabic with my mother. Proud-looking men in long coats and turbans knocked on my grandfather's door and attended his Sunday 'at homes'. The table in the hall was always loaded with different headgear. Those who spoke Arabic, Armenian or Turkish usually kept their headgear on. The ones speaking English or French left their hats in the hall. Five times a day we could see from our terrace the muezzine of the nearest mosque climbing into the round balcony of his minaret to deliver the call to prayer. As he moved slowly round, pausing to utter the call, he looked to us hardly larger than a puppet but his voice sounded surprisingly loud, even in those days without electric amplifiers. We were constantly being told we must learn Arabic. To encourage us, a little Arabic-speaking playmate was ordered to come to tea after she finished school every afternoon. Unfortunately, she was more strong-minded than us – she learned English but we did not learn Arabic. I now think we should have gone at least part time to local schools. I should not have been so lonely.

Between the wars, Syria was under French mandate so we heard French spoken in every possible kind of accent. We had French lessons from a cultivated couple, M. et Mme Baurain. In 1930, Paul Baurain published *Alep autrefois, aujourd'hui*, printed at the Maronite Press, Aleppo. The book, bound in striped silk made in Aleppo, is an artifact with its portraits of women long dead ('Type de grande dame Alepine') its advertisements for businesses, a very few of which still survive, and a map done in 1930 by the author himself which looks strangely empty.

When the Turkish gold sovereigns piled up in the safe in Black Grandpa's bedroom so that it could hold no more, he decided that it was time to start building a house for us all on a piece of land he owned near the hospital and the church. My mother said it was to be in what was then the chicken run. I did not believe her, the place was so smelly and full of droppings. But very soon the chickens – and the smell – vanished and the air was filled with the chip-chipping of the stonemasons, shaping and smoothing the huge pile of beautiful cream-coloured stones constantly being unloaded off strings of very cross camels.

These camels looked so fierce and ugly when forced to kneel down, groaning and moaning, their lascivious lips dripping green saliva and their huge teeth so very yellow, that I was sure they never cleaned them. The stonemasons were dressed in clean white, including their turbans, because everything got covered in a fine white bloom from the stone chipping. Very soon I knew where my bed was going to be, and the flights of stone steps were no longer perilous because the carpenters had made banisters. The work must have gone on through the summer because we came back from the mountains that year – 1926 – to find the house ready to move into. A stone fortress! The two upper floors were ours and the huge terraces, as big as rooms, looked out over the Muslim graveyard and the old town. As the roof was flat and balustraded, we could play there too and put out our beds when it got too hot, although this was barred to us in the rainy season when the cistern was collecting all our drinking water for the summer. My mother grew all sorts of English flowers on our terrace, including the only daffodils in the land. I remember her wonderful bulb catalogues. Black Grandpa, like most Armenians, did not know exactly when his birthday was, but we celebrated it on 21 March, the first day of spring, and there were always daffodils by his plate. His half of the house was downstairs with a connecting door between and we shared the garden. From 1926 until 1959, the road between us and the hospital was called Sharia Altounyan. Our playroom windows looked over to the hospital wards so that we provided mutual entertainment for each other in those pre-soap-opera days.

Poche is a name that occurs often in Black Grandpa's little diary and it was Dr Adolph Poche we used to tease and flirt with most afternoons as he worked with the X-ray. Until the end of his life he lived in one of the merchant khans in the souk which had been in his family since 1539, when the first Venetian merchants had arrived. He only moved out in 1987, a few months before he died at the age of ninety. His complicated lineage included Venetian consuls, French merchants, refugees from the Napoleonic Wars and the adopted daughter of a 'notable Christian family' long living in Aleppo. Adolph and his brother Rudolph were born in Aleppo. Adolph, a true Alepine, always chose his wives locally and never, apparently, thought of looking even as far as Damascus. He married first the widow of a British consul and, when she died, the sister-in-law of a British merchant who had found his wife in Aleppo. He gave his only daughter in marriage to a young Aleppo merchant and she is still there.

There was never any name or advertisement on either our house or our hospital; everyone knew where it was. And there was that strict European rule against doctors advertising, dinned into me in childhood, which has made me always distrust any form of advertisement. We children always enjoyed garish street signs: huge cut-outs of extracted teeth roots, complete with blood, over dentists' surgeries; or lurid scenes of birth over the house of the 'sage femme diplomé' (or midwife), a baby in a hugh bath, small enough to go down the plug-hole, neolithic-looking mothers in the act of giving birth – all in oil paints. We had to make the most of what we could find in these days before television. We were not usually allowed to go inside the cinema, so got what thrill we could out of the gigantic cut-out figures outside.

We were allowed to run free over most of the hospital, although not in the wards and the operating-room. What I saw once from a terrace, when an operating-room curtain happened to be left open, was enough to colour my nightmares for weeks. But there was always a welcome for us in the laboratories. The workers there, Eliza and Azniv, never seemed too occupied to let us squint down microscopes, play with the 'dear little dolls' stoves' used for Wassermann testing. The glass-fronted cupboards were full of gruesome toys, the relics of many years' operating – dried stomachs and unrecognizable parts of the body preserved in glass jars full of liquid. There was a foetus or two, I am sure, and, unless I am imagining, one of them two-headed – but it may have been a calf.

Ernest was in charge of the laboratory and one of the first things he had done after the war was to order about fifty guinea-pigs from Egypt and build a magnificent house for them with shady verandahs and special confinement huts, a lot more convenient than the hovels many of the Armenian refugees were living in. We did have an Armenian family to look after the animals – but it was good hospital work, helping to cure people. Perhaps they were not too resentful.

The kitchen, with its great mountains of food, was another playground. We were not allowed to bother the nurses when they were eating in the dining-room next door. Sometimes, we daringly went in through the patients' entrance, into the main waiting-room, and picked our way over families of bedouin squatting on the polished stone floors. We would hear whispers: 'There goes the wife of the doctor. Oh no, it must be his daughter.' They seemed to treat the visit to the hospital as an outing for all the family and did not seem to mind how long they waited. The X-ray room was open to us and no rules about keeping away from dangerous rays. In the semidarkness, we would watch the barium meal being swallowed and circulating along luminous intestinal passages. There was always work for us in the dispensary, rolling pills or spooning powders into rice-paper sachets big enough for a horse to swallow. The dark room was a pleasant change from the sun-glaring streets outside. At the engine-room door waited fat Antranik who had a story to tell us and sometimes – sometimes – would let us into the very dangerous engine room to watch the big wheel going round. If all else failed, there was Grandpa's kitchen or ours, but that was a bit too near home.

Everywhere people were only too glad to have a game, to be distracted, to forget the horror they had just been through. All were the remnants of the vast mass of Armenians deported from eastern Turkey, the only survivors from the massacres. My grandpa did his best to employ as many as possible and very rarely dismissed anyone. I remember a very clumsy waiter we had who was like a twisted tree standing by our table in a permanent dream – or nightmare. We used to tease him when the grown-ups were not there. But I think he had only just been saved from drowning in the Euphrates after a journey from his native hills, an even more horrible story than usual. Our cook with the cast in her eye and a fay grin, who went into such a panic at the sound of my father's knock on the front door; the girl in the laboratory, with a limp, so stunted that she could hardly reach the counter; the grotesquely tall chemist whose fez made him look even taller and who could not talk without stammering; the bony old lady ironing away all day in the dark basement of the hospital – all these were survivors and all smiled at us children and bore us thankfully.

When they were settled into their spacious flats, one above the other, Ernest and Black Grandpa lived very different lives. Although they worked side by side all day long in the hospital, they went home to two entirely separate lifestyles.

Upstairs, our booklined drawing-room, with its comfortable chintz-covered armchairs and sofa (for years I had never seen delphiniums except on upholstery), might have been Bloomsbury or Cambridge, as English spring visitors noted sometimes with surprise. In summer the shutters were left wide open and the hot wind rattled the pictures on the walls and laid a soft bloom of red dust over everything. My mother considered any moving air fresh, even if it seemed to come out of an *oven*.

> A scorching hot wind is blowing the house inside out. It is ninety degrees if you shut the shutters. We have our dinner on the terrace. We have discovered that we can see the screen of an open air cinema with field glasses and watch the blood curdling dramas full of shooting and motor cars.

The hot Aleppo nights were always full of the sound of brass music from the open-air café bands and the shouting and singing of people unable to sleep in the heat.

Downstairs, Black Grandpa's house was dark as a church with all the shutters tightly closed, from before sunrise, to imprison the cool night air and keep the dust out. In the winter, his walls were covered with carpets, his floors too and some of his sofas as well. There were no books to be seen, only large rolls of *The Times*, from months back, piled up beside the main armchair like logs. In the end they were all slit open with the silver paper-knife for the news about what was happening in Germany, Turkey, Syria, Lebanon and perhaps sometimes America. England and France were not so very important to my grandfather in those days. He secretly thought Germany should win the next war (if there was one) because she had lost the last. He admired Germany and, of course, he knew that country well, having spent many years at various laboratories there. The only other printed papers were medical books and journals which were all conscientiously and sometimes derisively read. He was not always respectful of European medicine. There were no bookshelves because there were no books to put in them. I used guiltily to enjoy the cool, different luxury of my grandfather's house. Sometimes, I slipped down to the dining-room where the two doctors were having a very late lunch and listened to details of their operations. I said nothing so as not to be noticed. My grandfather's dining-table was of shiny polished wood as my mother had at last persuaded him that cloths were out of fashion, but I don't think he really liked eating off 'bare boards'. When he had parties there was always a starched damask tablecloth. Upstairs we ate off bare oak and my mother had even had the varnish scraped off that.

On Sunday afternoons in winter, when it was too wet and cold to go sailing, or riding, the wood stove roaring in one corner and Dora sitting in another quietly reading or writing, and all the patients in the hospital, even the bad ones, unexpectedly recovering, Ernest would sit at his huge Underwood typewriter and write long, often miserable letters to his friends in England. He used only two fingers, his little finger crooked. The air would be hazy with smoke from his pipe and, as he thought, an idle hand would twist a black curl. His ribbon was a virulent purple colour and the lines were close together – to save postage! JR would get letters complaining:

> I have no wish to put it across this unspeakable people, this crooked clientel. I feel depressed at my ability to be solvent in my middle age working with people I am out of sympathy with, facing with frantic fury a milieu that is definitely hostile. From earliest childhood I have always hated Aleppo and am filled with gloom each time I see again those sterile hills.

Perhaps he did think he hated Aleppo, in contrast to the pleasure of being in England, and seeing his friends, but I wonder if he would have been happy to work permanently there. Whatever he might say, Ernest was fond of the patients, especially the 'disadvantaged' and the children. I have watched him reassuring a bedouin with wild and frightened eyes, perhaps on his first visit to a hospital, or calming a child. There was no doubt that he was happy to be able to help them. Most of the nurses loved him although, some mornings, they must have felt they were treading through minefields. Few people understood that Ernest was too vulnerable for his own comfort. A lot of his fierceness and bluster was a cover-up for deep hurt and uncertainty.

The two doctors disagreed on one very important point. It was a question of ethics. With Ernest there was never any doubt about operating on a dangerously ill patient if there was the slightest hope of saving his life. My grandfather's more cautious policy on this had been forged in hard times when not only his reputation but his life might have been at risk if the patient died. He would never operate if there was the slightest doubt about its success. Ernest had to feel that he had done every last thing – and he always minded desperately when a patient died. He never learnt to accept death, felt guilty, as if it was his fault. He never forgot 'that appalling first month at the Middlesex when I assisted at the death of one a day. I have frequently to face a corridor full of relatives with the announcement that the op has proved a post mortem – and it gets no easier with time!' Sometimes, I would be woken by the hospital telephone in the middle of the night. I knew by his voice that someone had just died. It made me feel sad and at the same time relieved to be alive.

Ernest believed that there must always be absolute honesty in dealing with a patient – even if the truth was unpleasant. (We children complained that sometimes when he told us it was going to hurt we screwed ourselves up for nothing.) This was an unfashionable attitude in Aleppo.

> There seems to be an extraordinary idea abroad that the patient is immortal until suddenly struck down by a ruthless doctor. So, when the outcome is uncertain, the doctor assumes a mask of inane bonhomie. Of course the patient knows when he is dying. He is facing reality with every fibre of his body. The relatives may flutter about distracted with grief but he can look to his doctor, familiar

with death, to stand by and assure him that what is happening is a normal process, normal since the beginning of time . . . Humanity stumbling through the valley of the shadow needs trusty guides, craves deeply for honesty.

There must be absolute honesty about *everything*: the patient's ulcers or his wife's sterility. He poured scorn on an incredible medical opinion current at the time, that in fertility cases the husband should not be examined because if he was found to be at fault, he might commit suicide.

In 1933, the *Lancet* published an article by Ernest entitled 'The Philosophy of treatment' ('the guts of my being', he called it). He attacks the 'mumbo-jumbo' (one of his favourite words) with which doctors surround themselves:

A horrid metamorphosis seems to occur when the medical student enters into practice. For five years he has been marching surefooted with gallant comrades along the macadamed road of anatomy, physiology, pathology . . . then suddenly the road ends and those surefooted ranks are transformed into flocks of frightened fowl scattering over the marsh of general practice, squawking in competitive panic on a thousand different notes. What are they up to? One thing is certain, we do not know ourselves . . . we stand before the public as purveyors of facts about the body. As a rule a patient comes to us because he wants to be cured. Suppose he has a fractured femur. Fractures have occurred since the beginning of bone life . . . Yet we cling to the magic of diversity. Home remedies are not enough, with pantomimic suddenness magic enters. Voices are hushed, the doctor takes out a pad of peculiar paper, the family follows anxiously the scratching of the professional pen.

He was against the doctor's monopoly of patent medicines. The London *News Chronicle* thought it worth a small paragraph: 'Surgeon thrusts at doctors. Mumbo-jumbo in the sick room.' 'I hope I shall not lose cast with my peers. I am now sending a thoroughly humdrum contribution about anaemia which I trust will rehabilitate me', Ernest wrote.

Ernest trained as an ear, nose and throat surgeon, and although, in Aleppo, he had to do almost everything, his 'hobby' was bronchoscopy: 'Little things please little minds and little things which go the wrong way into the bronchi or stick the right way into the stomach have always fascinated me'. In his early days in Aleppo, he was particularly proud of the new 'oesophagoscope' with its little light on the end. 'From everywhere over the horizon there have appeared specialists brandishing in their hands tubes . . . each and every one having at its end a small bright light.' With this they could now explore the human body until then 'opaque and largely dark'. With this and radiography they could examine without having to operate. In 1927, 'the pathology of the living' was ushering in an 'age of light'. Doctors would no longer be at the mercy of lab boys. 'Undreamed of possibilities' waited in the future now that a doctor could explore the dark tunnels of the body himself. Fishing objects out of the tunnels became his hobby – Ernest identified easily with children and it was children who most often swallowed things. 'A cheap glass bead more precious to me than any ruby'; 'a Turkish sovereign bright as the day it was minted'; 'a piece of well-used chewing gum'; 'a melon seed'; 'an overcoat button' – were all successfully fished out and made into a small paragraph in the *Lancet* or *British Medical Journal*. 'Two small coins were removed from a boy aged four. The X-ray showed one coin but the father said, "my child swallowed two coins. I heard them chink inside." He was right. (Always listen to what parents have to say!)'

One little girl from a mountain village had a piece of scrub oak lodged in her windpipe. 'She told me exactly what had happened: she was sitting swinging her legs on a branch while her brother told her funny stories. The leaf was between her lips, she drew in her breath to laugh and nearly choked to death.' The parents at once saddled a horse and set out for the Altounyan Hospital, not forgetting to cut a large branch from the tree. Another little girl came in who had been whooping for days. She had a piece of a toy trumpet lodged inside her. Some of the grown-up patients caught the doctor's imagination too. For example, there was the Kurd who had received a bullet in his lung – at Gallipoli. He had lived a quiet life until he began coughing blood ten years later. Then there was the old woman who had swallowed a sheep's ear while enjoying the popular Armenian sheep's head soup, *patcha*. And then there were the small children who drank caustic soda; it looked so like water there on the floor beside the squatting washwoman – such a temptation in the heat of summer. My father had devised a special method of gradually freeing the burnt throat, pulling a string a little further out day by day. So there were almost always naughty little boys running about the wards with string hanging out of their mouths.

Ernest hated 'mumbo-jumbo' of any kind, even when it was going to save trouble. Though he complained all the time about having to be a doctor, he was secretly idealistic. 'Sympathy for humanity, a passion for science', he told the graduating class of the Aleppo College, 'are the qualities needed to become a doctor and the third thing you will require is a persistent and unfailing courage. If you have not this, you have chosen wrong and will be of no possible use to Medicine, Humanity, or Yourselves.'

Ernest also enjoyed organizing the Near East Medical Association which met every year in various towns and provided a handy excuse for a spring holiday. Most of the members were missionary doctors and, of course, he could not resist stirring them up at times. 'Prayer is one of the most deadly weapons I know', he declared, opening a debate on 'Christianity and the cure of disease'.

> It means the surrender of human effort and generates an incredible amount of sloppy thinking. If prayer can bring about miraculous cures why bother about clinical exactitude? The worst about miracles is that they cannot be repeated. Doctors and clergymen can meet over a friendly cup of tea but heaven help us if we coincide over the prostrate body of the sick.

Black Grandpa had remarried in 1928 and, although Ernest's stepmother might be 'an enigma', she was also a well-trained nurse straight out from England, with whom he could talk professionally. Although her 'mousing about the house' ways irritated him, she was the best he had got to help him in his precious nursing school. The nursing school was the one thing the old doctor left entirely to his awkward son, 'which fills me with a bleak joy'. His dream was of a swarm of highly trained young ladies issuing yearly 'with a whirr of starched linen'. He might call them 'little donkeys' and make them cry, but he was also fond of them and proud when they graduated. His material was very rough indeed: all the girls were orphans from the Turkish massacres and, as he put it, 'the hereditary enemy of 75% of our patients'. It would not do to spoil them:

> We must provide something better, but not much better than they are used to. Nursing requires a practical mind and we must be careful in our attempts to broaden it not to lose touch with reality. If a girl has never slept off the floor it would be disastrous suddenly to provide her with a boudoir. If she has been addressed as something only a little better than an animal, it would cause too much mental confusion to give her the title of 'a lady on a visit from Europe'. A nurse's duty is to make the patient comfortable, not to cure him. I don't want to be told the specific gravity of his urine but how much egg he has eaten for breakfast.

No wonder he made them cry and some of them thought it better to do embroidery quietly at home and wait for marriage. They must be content to train girls who 'would naturally be cooks and children's maids'. The middle-aged should not be despised, 'though starched linen looks best on a trim figure'. He was not certain they had been right to insist on English-speaking students because they had lost some promising material that way. How he proposed to train them to pass written exams is not clear. Which of the five languages were they to use? And he could not help thinking that the woman of over forty, who could neither read nor write nor tell the time, nor, apparently, count above ten, was better than all the 'diploma-ed misses' for looking after his most precious instruments. No wonder some of the 'starched' matrons, out from England soon left 'in high dudgeon'. But the Altounyan nursing school did manage to turn out three or four passably trained girls every year. Dora designed the silver badge they all wore with a green enamelled shamrock in memory of Harriet Riddall.

Chapter Six

My mother tended to despise nurses unless they were interested in 'something else', such as art or music, and she kept a strict iron curtain between the house and the hospital. She scolded my father if he came home with so much as a spot of blood on his summer whites, although she could do nothing about the great clouds of ether smell that billowed out of him as he wearily climbed our two long flights of stone stairs, shouting for food at the end of the morning. I did resent the way she banged on the table as soon as the conversation became 'interesting', in other words medical: 'That's quite enough, dears'.

My grandfather had been a widower since Harriet had died in Ireland in 1907, and while he was building and organizing his hospital, and then building his house, he had not the time nor the money to think of replacing her. Countless matrons must have seriously set their caps at him. Now, in his old age, he was still physically lively and, what is more, reputedly rich. It was obvious to Aleppo society, although not to his family, that the old doctor needed someone to share his beautiful new house, someone not too intellectual, who could discuss patients and operations with him – even at table. So the town was well prepared for what happened next.

We knew my grandmother at Lanehead was not expected to live very much longer and, in fact, she died while we were in England in 1928. After the funeral, my parents went off to Vienna where my father was to visit some laboratories, leaving us at the farmhouse near Lanehead in the care of our nurses and a long-suffering cousin. Just before we had left Aleppo, a new sister tutor named Louisa (usually called Peggy) had arrived to work at the nurses' training school, Ernest's pet project. During the startling months to come we all kept in our minds our first picture of this person, dressed in blue velvet, curled up so prettily on the bear skin in front of my grandfather's 'English' log fire, in his bookless Maples drawing-room. She had seemed much too shy to speak, let alone to be plotting anything. And now here was my mother back from Vienna – alone. When she broke the news the earth seemed to open beneath our feet: 'Black Grandpa has married Miss D'. Black Grandpa who, for us, was as permanent as the Aleppo Castle, had done this thing, married a nurse who was presumably now to be our grandmother! We had seen her before we left – a girl barely older than us. We felt betrayed as well as startled. And my father felt hurt as he rushed back to Aleppo by the first tramp steamer from Athens (there was no faster way). He was hurt not to be in his father's confidence, and he might well have been jealous. And, at the back of his mind, was perhaps a faint hope that here was an excuse to leave Aleppo. After more than eight years there, he and Dora were not yet certain that they wanted to stay. 'We are both getting older and soon it will be too late to make a fresh start', Dora wrote. 'Syria is such a muddle that it is not a place in which to bring up a family.'

My father arrived just too late for the wedding, but in the bare twenty-four hours he spent with her (he couldn't bear her company any longer than that) he made up his mind that his new stepmother was a 'bad lot'. Greed for money could be the only reason a farmer's daughter would marry an old man three times her age. And in those days 'farmer' meant 'farm labourer'. Ernest informed the young woman that his father had no money at all – this he half believed himself! Back at Lanehead, he sent off an 'ultimatum', threatening to sell out – whatever that meant. The old man was not impressed. He knew that Ernest would never be able to keep a wife and five children in England without his help. And Ernest was, after all, interested in the new nursing school even if he had to start it with the assistance of his stepmother.

After Christmas at Lanehead, the caravan set out again and got to Aleppo in spite of snow and landslides:

> I found my father blooming in all directions and apparently very happy and I have had a long straight and not too violent talk which seems to have settled things in principle, and as much as can be expected in practice. . . . One thing emerges from this turmoil I can never leave Aleppo again for years and years.

For a time things went well and, in spite of a humiliating operation for haemorrhoids which, with his usual exaggeration, made him moan that he would never survive his father, Ernest seems to have been fairly ebullient:

> The old man is going from strength to strength. I see him once a day and say good morning and good evening to him and his wife, and for the time being that is all that is possible. To me she is an enigma to which I am prepared to give the benefit of the doubt.

And, with his maddening mock-modesty, he wrote: 'I am plodding ignominiously in the rear and making frequent applications for pocket money'.

After his marriage, Black Grandpa's reputation in Aleppo became even greater. He had proved that he was still young. Ernest wrote:

> His star is burning with dazzling glory, he has smashed up all opposition and proved to the richest of the land that there is no god but god and his name is A.A.A. . . . I have separated my own work from his and we meet in solemn consultation at the patient's bedside. My one bright experience since I returned has been the fishing out or tickling out of renal calculus from the urethra without a cutting operation. This can only rarely have occurred before in the history of surgery and is not likely to occur again with me.

Soon after Black Grandpa's remarriage, Aleppo thought it was time to celebrate his 'Fifty Year Jubilee' in 1930 – fifty years since he graduated from Aintab College in 1880. His old tutor, Dr Siouni who had taken him to Aintab, was there to vouch for the date. He was even older than Black Grandpa!

Ernest could not help enjoying the grand ball, the finest ever held in Syria, he boasted to his friends in England:

> Two hundred guests dancing in a pink pavilion with mirrors on the ceiling to an orchestra. Fountains flowing with coloured water, and unlimited champagne. Continued till the lights paled in the trees in the dawn, only interrupted at midnight by a cabaret of Hungarian dancers.

I remember it was my thirteenth birthday, so I was allowed to stay up late – to the envy of my sisters who could only watch the dancing through the stair railings. I wore a long blue dress, a white velvet flower in my hair, and grown-up men asked me to dance.

Black Grandpa still had twenty full years to live after his jubilee.

Chapter Seven

IN JUNE, when Aleppo got too hot to bear, we always moved to the mountains until October. We were to lose this haven.

Souookolook was an Armenian village on a spur above the bay of Alexandretta (or Iskenderun, as it is now known), in the extreme north-east corner of the Mediterranean. Our house and estate was on another mountain spur well away from the noisy village. The long, low house hugged the line of the hill, unobtrusive as a group of bedouin tents, and we children had a whole hillside, and a valley, as our playground. From our verandah we could see across the bay into the Forbidden Land, where our grandfather was born, and where neither he nor any of us could go because of our Armenian surname. We could see to where the road ran along the coast to the frontier. We watched the evening sun flush on the Taurus mountains, rising like a wall between us and the land where the Armenians came from. It would have taken hardly a day to travel to all those cities of magic – and horror – Maras, Aintab, Urfa, Diarbekir; Sivas would have taken a few hours longer.

As a child, Ernest used to come north to the same mountains. In those days, when it was all part of the Ottoman Empire, the whole family would move out of Aleppo in a caravan – horses and carriages, donkeys and mules, carrying with them all that was necessary for three months: household goods, bedding, tents, food. The infant Ernest and his sister Norah travelled in paniers on either side of a stalwart mule, dozing and waking when they were hungry to pick at the pile of bread and cheese tied on to the saddle between them. The ladies travelled with my grandmother in the carriage and so did the female servants.

My grandfather, independent on his fine horse, ranged here and there. Most of the tinned food had been ordered from Morton's in London months before. Sometimes the kitchen stores got confused with the toiletries – once my grandfather's favourite Pears soap got served up as jelly.

So when the two doctors closed the hospital, we got a taste of the old days and went camping for a week or ten days in the mountains above the village where we had our house. Not an hour's ride away was a magic land where the earth was a different colour and the trees were different and much larger. In this new land were giants' graves at least twenty feet long, springs so cold they would crack a water melon, snowpits where the snow was packed hard in the winter under layers of dead leaves and branches. Before fridges were common, in the heat of July and August we watched great blocks of compacted snow sawn out and carried, dripping on donkey-back, to cool the drinks of the Alexandrenes ten miles away.

Most exciting of all, there were wild boars. We were tired of hearing stories of wild-boar hunts in the winter, when deep snow lay over everything and we were cooped up in Aleppo. Snow! In Sivas villages we heard it used to come up to the eves of the houses. I would wrongly imagine three-storey houses. In Coniston, in the winter, we enjoyed sledging and wept at the agony of cold toes. But wild boar! We were always looking for their tracks, listening for the sound of movement in fields of corn, hearing the story of how one had rushed through Hovsep's legs – it would have turned and savaged him if he had not put in a clever shot. And, at last, one night when we were all sleeping in trees round the snowpit, one bright moonlight night with Orion swinging overhead, suddenly there were shouts: 'Wake up! Come down! They have shot a wild boar!' Smaller than we had imagined, but with tusks gleaming in the moonlight, and *new* stories about narrow escapes. I have never tasted meat so good as the kebabs we had that day.

When they were not going on and on about wild boar, our friends Hovsep and Garabet were talking about rocks: the Honey Rock, the Burning Rock – 'only a few hours' ride away'. We never saw the Honey Rock but it was easy to imagine.

The Unknown Remembered Gate

Every morning at breakfast we spread our paper-thin bread with white, homemade goat's butter and wild honey. It came to us in petrol tins, always exciting to dip into. You had to spoon carefully as there was a choice between the dark and the blond, tasting so different. Sometimes you got a mouthful of something really nasty – old wax or a crushed bee? But the Burning Rock. My father listened intently, sucking his pipe. I imagined a rock, flaming, suspended in the air.

Donkeys, mules and horses gathered at our front gate and off we set along the sea coast. The way was difficult – up hill and down dale, over rough country. Sometimes I had to get off my mare and slide with her down the side of a steep valley; sometimes I found myself dragging at the reins, hauling her up behind me. At last we reached the very tip of the promontory. There was the Burning Rock – slightly disappointing but certainly burning, more like a gas jet, coming out of a rather small crack in the rock. We could easily blow it out but it ignited again at once.

We created new legends as we wandered in the uninhabited hills, pitching our white tents for the night, when possible in reach of water. One morning, we woke to find wild Turkoman men sitting in a circle round us, waiting to see what sort of people we were and if we were alive. They had hoped to find a crashed aeroplane perhaps.

Each summer Roger made larger and larger kites until they were taller than himself, and needed yards and yards of string to fly. Those very fragile octagons of tissue paper, bamboo and homemade paste, sometimes over six feet across, were sent on adventures high into the clouds where we could not go. He threaded circles of paper onto the string and watched the 'message' fly up to the kite. Sometimes he got bored and handed the string to the ubiquitous little boy who would tie it to a blackberry bush while he tried to bring down a bird with his catapult. When the string broke, there it was going up into the mist with nothing on the end – no kite. This was a wonderful excuse to set off after it through the pinewoods on the other side of our fence, through uncharted country, down into the next valley, dank and dark and dripping where the ferns grew lush. Was it really inhabited by a huge snake or a black scorpion or perhaps a wolf? On the dusty paths, threading through the scrub, we seemed to meet people of a kind we had never seen before, dressed in strange costumes, a new kind of fez on their heads, speaking a strange new language which might have been Kurdish. We felt grown-up when they saluted us seriously and asked us to their homes. Sometimes they had found our kite, perhaps it had plummetted on to a flat roof, scattering red peppers or boiled corn spread out to dry. Sometimes it had even knocked someone down – a toddling baby perhaps. They had never in their lives seen such a kite.

Before our father made a swimming pool for us in our valley, we used to venture as far as 'The Shepherd's Pool'. It was a hot and sweaty walk and we were by no means sure of a welcome. We always stopped at the point where the path led steeply down to the huge rock overhanging the natural pool – and listened. If we could hear goat bells, shouts and splashes, the sounds of flutes, or large stones falling about, then shepherds were in possession – best go home again. But I learned to swim in that pool, felt the first delirium of floating, never mind that the ground round about was strewn with goat droppings and there were always watchers in the shadows. The shepherd boys were braver than us and dived fearlessly off the high rock, although their splashy swimming was not quite 'right'.

There were said to be bears in these mountains. The pelt of the last one shot had been given as a present to my grandfather and was in his drawing-room in front of his log fire. In winter there *were* wolves, too, but those cries we heard in the night were only hyenas and jackals. Souookolook nights were full of animal noises; humans went to bed early.

There was plenty to do inside our fence within the sound of our dinner gong. Our own vineyard, a few yards from the house, may not have produced grapes fit for my grandfather's table (the two gardeners had other things to do and did not tend it as well as they should have) but the semiwild grapes hidden in weeds were honey-sweet and good to sustain a long afternoon spent basking on a hot red earth slope with a book. My father spent some of his holiday energy in planning and helping to dig a tennis court and a swimming pool: 'the water gurgles and the pines wave and you see the gulf of Alexandretta while you serve from the cliff end'. Hunting for a lost ball might take us a long way down towards the distant sea.

Near the tennis court was a water tank for the tomato gardens. Its square, smooth, concrete top, on which the tennis parties used to sit and have tea, gave my mother an idea. She remembered her father's plasticine and papier-mâché models of the Lake District, and set out to help us model a map of the Middle East, including Turkey, the Forbidden Land – in mud on top of the tank. We were always making mud. Breathing hard, squatting, our bare brown knees up to our chins, we modelled mountains, smoothed deserts, made depressions for lakes, referring all the time to our tattered and stained school atlas. Trains of ants would wander across our plateaux, grasshoppers landed on our airstrips, stray grains of corn suddenly sprouted like tiny green poplar trees. When the sun was low, our miniature ranges of mountains threw long, real shadows and flushed pink with the real Taurus across the bay.

Souookolook was an Armenian village and had been so for a very long time. They spoke a special dialect among themselves which we could not understand. They had had to leave their homes more than once during the massacres and deportations. Most of the survivors had come back to start new families. There were few old people. We had survivors living on our land to look after it while we were not there, and their children were our playmates in the summer. A little further down the hill was a family we used often to go and spend the day with. They were richer than our gardeners because they owned property, were yeoman farmers. They had a few fields, a few orchards, some vineyards, a few cows, goats, sheep – they were self-supporting, hardly employing any labourers and doing the work themselves. All the summer was spent gathering stores for the winter and we used to 'help' them with the grapes, the walnuts, and making *pekmez* which is a sort of syrup of molasses made out of grapes. They came to visit with baskets of hard peaches covered with vine leaves, or tins of honey. As their property was a little further down the hill, their tomatoes ripened first and they had the best apples. We bathed in their 'pool' – its real purpose was irrigation, not merely for play like ours (all that water going to waste). The late autumn was always a race with bad weather, the monsoon-strength gales which battered the unharvested walnuts, washed away tomato fields and, what was much worse for us, threatened to destroy the road. In the early days before macadam, the lovely days between the storms tempted us to stay on and on while our retreat road down the mountain crumbled.

We always expected to come back the next year – if we were not at Lanehead. Then a new shadow began to grow, to threaten our paradise, our place of refuge. It first began as rumours. The evening gatherings on our terrace began to ask anxious questions. Was it true that the land was going to be given to the Turks? Nightmares began again. Should they all have to leave – for a third time? Would there be more killing and deportation? No more talk about wild boar or magic rocks. What are the Turks going to do now? What will they do to us?

The rumours were true. France had made an agreement with Turkey to return the sanjak of Alexandretta, which had been part of the mandate allotted to France in 1920. In 1938, war with Germany was becoming a probability. Turkey had fought on Germany's side during the 1914 war. It was hoped that this time she would at least be neutral.

As we made our Sunday journeys to Souookolook we watched the signs. At first it seemed as though the sanjak would be autonomous. The flags on the green triumphal arches over the road were not the usual Turkish flag but had the star and crescent outlined only. But each week there seemed to be more and more real Turkish flags – and we had to wait longer and longer at the frontier which up till then had been a formality. Our passports were sometimes examined by soldiers who obviously did not know how to write but just copied the outlines of the words into the necessary spaces on their forms. Ernest firmly advised leaving. Memories of the past were too strong. Eventually, although there were no massacres this time, most of the Armenians left. Once again Aleppo received refugees.

It was heartbreaking to visit our friends in their cramped rooms, sitting with nothing to do, no fields to till, no fruit to gather, no animals to feed. The young men who had been used to herding sheep and goats found jobs as motor mechanics.

The Unknown Remembered Gate

Their mothers swept and cooked and tried to keep their pitiful surroundings clean. Their idle men sat running their beads through their fingers and wondering what was going to happen next. Sometimes they managed to slip back for a day or two and wandered round their deserted houses, their unhoed lands, cursing and spitting. They had been on good terms with the Turkish villagers. Now the few Armenians who had elected to stay behind seemed suddenly more unfriendly than the Turks. I remember how they avoided our eyes, tried not to see us. And we began to go less and less to Souookolook, which was now inhabited by ghosts. Our trees grew tall, our roofs fell in, our tennis court was for drying bulgar on and our swimming pool made a useful washing place. Now we could sympathize with so many of the Armenians who had lost all they had time and again. We still never talked about what had happened a quarter of a century ago but it never ceased to reverberate, to trouble us in our dreams.

Ernest, loath to give up anywhere he had loved, wrote to his friends:

> We still try to go there when we can. It is too lovely for words. The house is now almost hidden by the growth of trees, the path to the house is a leafy tunnel. Water trickles into cool pools. Wild boar spoors are visible all over the grounds. We hope to make it habitable again. I can take my own car and chauffeur whenever I like. The swimming pool and tennis court are intact.

I always asked first about the swimming pool and the tennis court. I did not really care if the roof was falling in. But we never went there again. I felt lonely without our Armenian friends.

Chapter Eight

IMAGINED FROM hot and dusty Aleppo, Lanehead was always under rain. And, sure enough, when we arrived in the huge hired Daimler, the laurels by the front door were varnished with wet and dripped on us as we pushed through the little iron gate, the creak and clang of which has been ever in our dreams since our last visit. In my memories, yellow iceland poppies, bowed with raindrops, are bright against the funeral gloom of the dark front door half hidden between tall black yew trees. The door bell sounds many miles away in the depths of the house, and it seems an age before we hear approaching footsteps. When the door is unbarred at last the hall is so dark that we cannot see where to put our bags. We feel our way by memory and instinct. A strong smell of oil-paint as the study door opens, and White Grandpa stands against a shaft of light. We all crowd into the morning-room where Granny waits. She is, of course, smaller than we remember because we have grown. Behind her, bowls of roses and sweet peas are reflected in polished wood. When we are small, the flowers are outlined against the fir trees in the garden and on the mountain on the other side of the lake. But always the room is too vast to be taken in all at once.

Actually over the fireplace is a large window looking through the conservatory and right down the lake. We balance on the fender, warming the front of our legs while we consider the wind and whether it is fit for sailing. Still in our travelling clothes, we are soon out of the morning-room window and down the steep hill to the boathouse, returning only reluctantly to tea, cobwebs on our shoulders.

I always began the day hoping to sail and, if that was not

possible, to climb mountains. 'Peel Island days' were carefully spent like gold sovereigns. We recognized these days as soon as we woke up. A light morning haze over the mountains meant that it was going to be fine. There was a heavy smell of pine needles and hay as we went down to the lake, and the air was so still that you could hear the cows lowing in the fields, the cocks and hens in the farm, and even noises from the village on the other side of the lake. On a day like this there would certainly be a west wind which would take us down to the island, about four miles away, in one or two long tacks. Minnows flashed away as Roger got the boat out. *Swallow*'s brown sail hoisted, the landmarks slipped by easily enough. Fir Island is half-way. After that Peel Island, almost within touching distance, looks from the north like a green footstool on the water. On the east side the rock is sheer down to the water and the island is more like a battleship, with 'The Calf', the smaller island to the south, like an attendant cruiser. The Collingwoods and the Altounyans are not the only families who regard the island as theirs by rights. Five generations now have lit fires in that fireplace at the top of the cliff. But if we happen to find the island uninhabited, we can imagine that it is ours.

Though I must have met my 'Ukartha', as we children called Arthur Ransome, in Hampstead when I was only a few days old, I think we really got to know him as a family in the summer of 1928. By then we were aged eleven, nine, eight, six and two. It was an eventful time for all of us: we had a new baby sister after being a more or less self-contained family for years, and now our grandmother was very ill, perhaps dying. It was the first time we had met death in the family. I was very upset and cried loudly until told to stop by my mother. Uncle Arthur had just decided to give up working as a journalist on the *Manchester Guardian* and to try writing children's stories. Perhaps if we had not been in England that year we should never have been the 'Swallows'. Because our parents were otherwise occupied, we saw more of our adopted uncle. He and Aunt Genia, his wife, seemed always on the shore when we were 'messing about'. To put their minds at rest, Arthur and my father went off to Barrow together to buy the safest boats they could find. It would certainly take a lot to capsize *Swallow* or

Mavis. We never wore life-jackets but there was a rule against ever standing up in a boat until we could swim. I don't know how we managed to creep about on bended knees but I remember jumping in fully clothed to prove that I could swim. And we all learned fast. We also had a light rowing boat with long fixed oars which Roger rowed about a lot, looking rather like a water spider. I'm almost sure he could not swim. He was small and could not row sitting down.

When he had to go back to Aleppo, Ernest left the newly acquired *Swallow* in the charge of his good friend Arthur: 'I can see the crinkle of sail along the boom and I hope to god you hard-down your tack properly and don't pinch her when close hauled . . . write me something to make me smell the wind and the water again.' Less than two years later, on 18 July 1930, **Dora wrote:** '"Swallows and Amazons" arrived yesterday at 1 p.m. and it is now 6 a.m. There have been very few hours out of those eighteen when it has not been read by somebody . . . All I want to say is that we like it *enormously*.'

The family were badly in need of distraction that July. It was very hot, as usual. All day long a hot wind would blow from the west, 'blowing up dust and garbage and people's tempers until murder seems natural'. Black Grandpa and his new wife were away on a sea cruise, 'or we should have been in the hills long ago'. Ernest was faced with having to operate on his one and only son Roger, very ill with tonsillitis (no antibiotics had yet been invented): 'A very nasty job and I can tell you one that makes one feel like a murderer . . . But what is all this bleating about when all I want to tell you is that 'Swallows and Amazons' has arrived. D. and I sat up all night.

> We grabbed it from each other and the children took it in form order and devoured it with the same intensity that they suck oranges through sugar lumps . . . I especially like and marvel at your extraordinary accurate characterisation of the kids . . . damn fine sporting kids I think . . . and then I realise that they are *mine* . . . A most exhilarating experience . . . So long as Roger does not hop off on a decline I shall never regret having four girls. I certainly wanted an heir but one is quite enough . . . What

Brigit will say when she finds she has been labelled 'Vicky' I shudder to think ... Certain things in the book sent a tingle down my spine ... when the steamer hooted and Taqui blushed, for instance ... But oh this fiendish malignant wind that tears at the nerves.

Arthur was dissatisfied with his first illustrator. Dora disagreed with him:

Of course he hasn't the smallest idea of what mountains are ... to him they are no more than bits of crumpled paper ... but he's got the right angle to the rocks on Peel Island ... Don't go and imagine that I mean to insult the book by saying that the pictures are good enough for it ... I mean that the things in which the illustrations fall short are what nobody knows but *US* ... The kids send their love and all sorts of disrespectful messages.

The kids were indignant at being made to wear berets, but did not seem to mind when it was pointed out that the family in the book was very much tidier than they were.

By the time *Swallowdale* came out, our affection for Arthur, and his for us, was at its height. He was assured that book two was even better than book one. The gratified 'uncle' asked everyone for ideas on the next book. 'Swallows in Syria' was never written but many letters, by all the family except Roger and baby Brigit, were expended in urging him to come out to Syria to get ideas. ' "Swallowdale" is even better than "Swallows and Amazons" and you need not have been so pessimistic about it. I'm not going to write to you again until "Swallows in Syria" is in print,' I wrote.

I took my duties as editor of 'The Aleppo Mercury' very seriously and, when 'Ukartha' was in hospital, I thought he might just as well employ his time on 'something that will fill up space. And a few drawings would not be sniffed at ... Daddy had got the plans for the boat you sent him so I hope he will buck up and see if the local carpenter can turn out anything that will float.' We heard that 'The Queen' (Queen Mary) had been reading some of the letters we had written to our 'uncle', so we had to be careful: 'Well. This is a rubbishy letter. For goodness sake don't show it to any booksellers etc . . . Have you been snowed under by admirers? I'm sure this very letter will be flattened by many others addressed to you at Jonathan Cape.'

The Ransomes did finally come to Syria, bringing with them the little ten-foot dinghy I dreamed of but not the Norfolk wherry that my father had ordered:

> I want an absolutely sound hull and sail, the mast of course with counterweight and 'tabernacle', with two quants. I have decided that the Antioch swamp can only be tackled with one of these. Just let me know the price before you conclude the bargain – an old one which DOES NOT LEAK ONE DROP will do . . . You see I have just escaped being rather badly lost in the swamp. I got back last night and am still rather glad to be alive. But I am longing to go again and put in a few stakes here and there as guides.

Arthur settled down to work in Dora's studio at the top of the house. He was writing *Peter Duck*. At lunch time each day, he would come slowly down the stairs. We met him at the bottom: 'How many pages?' He would silently hold up different numbers of fingers and always repeat the refrain, 'And Genia thinks them *AWFUL*'. After lunch he would read them to us and we did all we could to cheer him up. In the afternoons we played tennis, not very well, and Uncle Arthur would play to us on his penny whistle, and tell us Annancy stories from the West Indies. We all got very fond of them both.

Then, suddenly, it was all over. We children had no idea why they left in such a hurry. I complained:

> To think that you spent or rather wasted a whole week puttering round Cyprus in an almost empty boat drives me mad. If only you hadn't gone off in such a dashed hurry I'm sure we could have persuaded daddy to let us go with you. I'm sorry I did not wave a damp hanky when you drove off . . . mine certainly was damp, but I was feeling too much of a donk to wave it. [Pure Captain Nancy language!]

Mavis wrote more calmly:

> You know I really think you need not have gone so soon and in such a hurry like that. You could have easily stayed another month, getting on with P.D., which really is getting – or was getting – on so nicely.

I think we were told that Arthur's Russian wife had been fussing that our aluminium pans would harm his ulcer. *We* thought it might have been because of the young tortoises we had brought home: 'Give my love to Aunt Genia and tell her that BOTH the tortoises were let out by the Roman arch BEFORE (N.B.) your letter was written.'

Dora writes coolly but one can feel the hurt under the polite style:

> It was so nice to hear from you at last and to know you were having a jolly time, though I must say it is rather tantalising to think of you having been almost within reach for so many days after you left . . . Nice of you to say such kind things about my painting. My sketches are potty little things. I think you exaggerate rather. I would never stand up against painters who do nothing else. I don't want to. I paint for fun . . . I don't know what to say about sending the children to school. It is such a terrible uprooting for one thing, and I hate to think of it. But we *are* thinking and perhaps will be able to decide something, some day.

That was the trouble. Ernest's letters were now long and angry. It almost seems as if a fight had developed for possession of the children – us. Arthur and Genia had perhaps began to suggest, tactfully they thought, what Ernest and Dora had already been talking about: that Aleppo was not the best place to educate children. Ernest took this as a reflection on the way he and Dora were bringing us up.

> Aleppo in Hell. 15.6.32.
>
> Your letter, straight from the shoulder, to an unmanly father of poor children who were not being given a chance was, I'm sure, well meant.

The term 'psychological bilge' is bandied to and fro. Arthur was never eager to have his inner feelings examined at the best of times. And old rivalries came to the surface: 'Whatever you think I only ask you to believe that D. and I are acting in agreement and I am not managing her in the least.' Whatever Arthur meant, Ernest took it that he was being blamed for keeping her out in the East too long. The children would feel like savages when next they landed in England and not be able to fit in . . . They would be behind other children of their age.

Ernest now swore that nothing on earth would make him go to England a moment earlier than he absolutely had to. The children had been doing yearly examination papers sent out from England and no complaints had been made about their standards. 'The future will of course show which of us is right. I cannot help thinking that the root of your objection to their upbringing is that they have been under my influence too long.' Genia probably took a hand in the argument (which must have gone on after we were all in bed) with Arthur and Dora looking miserable and not enjoying it at all. Genia and Ernest were both people who had to get their own way and, probably, Genia felt forced to 'sweep out' when she was defeated.

In the end ('nothing to do with the Ransomes') the decision was made to send us all to school 'because of the impossibility of their meeting others of their own age out here . . . Taqui has suddenly decided to try for a scholarship to Oxford'. And so I was sent to a 'homelike' boarding school where no one but an unfortunate girl with a bad heart had ever been known to pass an exam, mainly because the dormitory windows looked out on Windermere with a view of the famous Langdales where my parents had spent their honeymoon. My aunt Ursula knew the headmistress, and said she was a nice motherly woman.

Ernest was never one to sulk – he needed his friends too much:

I forgive you for all the hard things you tried to say. Please don't give me up . . . Although I shall be seeing you in a few days I cannot but write to say as day succeeds day perfectly in the mountains, the pool is hidden by the spray of falling bodies – Taqui the champion swimmer, Susie the champion diver, Titty [Mavis] diving with the utmost intellectual precision, Roger bravely swimming miles under water (though only just), and the tennis court resounds with the thwack and swish of hand driven balls ... when I see all this happening beautifully and exquisitely and for the last time for them, for they are, thank god, untouched by the vulgarity of Europe, which is in many ways worse than the vulgarity of the East, when, as I say, all this is happening, Dora and I with one deep sigh from the heart (Excuse Genia the mention of this wallowing organ.) we say 'oh dear if only Uncle Arthur and Aunt Genia were here ...' even if they did try to scold us for mysterious reasons too hard to discover. They alone can really drink with us the full flavour of the scene. SO THERE. I am coming to England for the last time, and hope to recapture the pleasure of the England I love (and excuse the intrusion – have bled for.)

This letter brings tears to my eyes, even now, sixty years later, but I can't help feeling that it may have been received at Low Ludderburn with sniffs and derision as 'more sentimental twaddle'.

Titty, writing after the beginning of term, seems to say it all: 'Here we are all dressed in green, learning our lessons like good little girls. So far, everything has gone all right, and I find that I am not at all behind other girls of my own age. . . . Bother I must stop and go out for a bally walk.'

The Ransomes were good to us poor exiles. At weekends, Arthur would turn up at the boarding school in his Trojan car to take us to their house at Low Ludderburn for the afternoon. More than once I had a migraine and spent the journey being sick into a can in the back. Ukartha was sympathetic but gruff: we had to 'buck our stumps' and not complain. Coming to school in England was supposed to toughen us up. I can imagine the sort of conversation they had after we had been taken back. Was there any hope for us?

After a year I did so much weeping in the headmistress's beautiful drawing-room, which we only saw when our parents visited us, that I was transferred to a day school in Cambridge. This was much better. I was actually allowed to work. My

English essays were appreciated. *Swallows and Amazons* still bugged me for a while. I was surprised that girls of my age, fourteen or fifteen, wanted to play those sort of games — especially as there were no boats in sight. I was much too busy trying to adapt to a new life and I did not need a sort of boy scout fantasy imposed. I felt a fraud. Very soon someone would find out that I was not in the least like 'Captain John'. If this was my only passport to acceptance in Cambridge, I preferred to do without it. The Walkers were certainly not the Altounyans. The father I knew would never have sent that telegram about 'duffers' even if he did aim to bring us up sportingly. Ukartha never meant the family to be exactly like us, he took our names and wrote the first book 'in return for a pair of slippers', because he was genuinely sorry for us having to leave the lakes and mountains he had loved so much all his life. It was not his fault that the books were so popular that we sometimes found ourselves pressured into acting the people that had our names. The stories were never meant to be studies of our true characters. In one letter I had from him when *Swallows and Amazons* first came out Ukartha wondered if we felt like dead butterflies stuck on cards in a collection or a stuffed perch in its glass case with artificial grass and painted water. But we did not. There were more tangled threads in the story of Ernest's friendship with Arthur than we were aware of — some of them never got sorted out! In its simplest terms, their suspicion of each other began with their competing for the love of the Collingwoods when they were young men.

White Grandpa died in 1932. I am shocked to find that I have no memory of this. Surely I would have howled even louder than I did when Granny died. But I was fifteen by then and probably overwhelmed by the reality of living in England — submerged in my own unhappiness. I hope he has forgiven me! His guide to the Lake Counties was published a few weeks before he died at Lanehead.

Chapter Nine

From the moment my parents first arrived in Aleppo it had been obvious that Ernest would never be able to work happily with his father. He could never settle for being a shadow, though at first he did try. My mother wrote home of an embarrassing 'incident' – 'most painful', she called it. The first time they went to church, 'one of the congregation stood up and pointed E. out as the son of etc etc . . . E. has not acquired the art of taking such things calmly and was extremely shy.' He wanted to sink into the ground, but no one in Cambridge or Lanehead would have called him shy. In Aleppo he pretended to be. He refused to compete with his universally charming father in any obvious way. But he had a secret area of his own which his father, who hardly ever read a book if it was not medical, could never invade.

Ernest wanted passionately to be a poet. His pride was that he could be an adequate surgeon as well, and do his job 'without killing anybody'. He wrote poetry during his periodic 'breakdowns', the first of which happened when he was quite young. 'My internal turmoil began at sixteen at Rugby', he told John Rickman. The initial shock of being sent away to school so young must have had repercussions all through his life. He was lucky to have been able to make friends who supported him. Marrying my mother was the wisest thing he ever did. But as he advanced into middle age he found life more and more difficult. After the jolt of his father's new marriage came the huge effort of parting from four of his five children when they went to school. Besides the every worrying expense (it cost a thousand pounds a year to keep four of us in England), our continued unhappiness must have reminded him of his own infant misery. 'Oh dear these children,' he wrote, 'it is as if one had projected pseudopodea of naked protoplasm for all the world to stamp on. I can only cope by resolutely switching off my mind from the subject ... a dash of brute courage usually enables me to get through.' A solution to the problem of the children was for Dora to stay for at least a term in England at Lanehead, which by that time my father had bought. Ernest was to join her the following Christmas.

As the hot lonely months of 1933 crept by, Ernest missed Dora more and more, and realized sadly that he would probably never again have the children rampaging round him. They would be changed, grown up. He could hardly bear it. 'I live for the morning post to bring me help but dread to open letters in case they bring me bad news', he wrote to John Rickman. He was 'on the brink of a long plunge through the waters of middle life'. Anyone could have foreseen what came next. The catalyst was an Australian girl on her way back home after a trip to Europe. In those days you could get off the Orient Express at Aleppo and put up at the Baron Hotel for a few days, and then continue by the next train. She probably did not realize the effect she had had on the lonely poetic doctor she met one evening over dinner at the hotel: 'I am experiencing a state far surpassing the state of twenty years ago. I have loved and been loved by someone who cell by cell is my complete counterpart.' One can imagine Dora receiving this letter at Lanehead. She was kept informed 'hour by hour' on all that happened and assured that she was loved more than ever. 'Whether it be necessary to turn Moslem or not (I am joking),' he wrote to his confessor John Rickman, 'I shall of course live with both of them. Dora reacted 'true as a steely mirror held to truth'.

The girl continued her journey and, as far as I know, did not answer the spate of letters and uninhibited poems that followed her home. Perhaps she sometimes looks at photographs taken in Aleppo and remembers. I shall never forget that strange Christmas when my father spent the time in manic dancing which I found very disturbing. Some of his friends took a different view. 'He is typing his poetry to jazz', wrote a

Cambridge friend, visiting Lanehead at the time, to John Rickman.

> He and the children dance gracefully together. He is as delightful a father as he ever was. Dora is accepting the situation with her usual gallantry and there is a sense of harmony, though sometimes difficult harmony, between them. Has he performed the miracle we poo poo-ed of warming her with his love for the other girl? He can do things in the way of personal relations – always could – which no one else seems capable of.

Whatever John Rickman might say about belated adolescence in a man 'more than ordinarily dependent on his wife and growing aghast at this dependence', Ernest was happily writing poetry. Verse poured out of him almost like automatic writing. He hardly ever altered a line. It was all neatly typed out by his secretary when he got back to Aleppo. Fortunately, she did not have enough English to understand it. In 1934, Ernest boasted to his Cambridge friends: 'T.E. poor devil, has his nose in my book. He has faithfully promised to spend two hours on it as soon as he is out of the airforce.' There was one person at least who Ernest felt could understand his poetry, and that was T.E. Lawrence. They had first met as young men in 1911. The archaeologist Leonard Woolley employed the young Oxford man that year on his spring dig at Carchemish near Aleppo. Ernest must have had time on his hands during his enforced year at Aleppo because of a nervous breakdown. In his vulnerable state any sympathy would have been like water in the desert. And 'TE' was probably glad to talk to him and use the Altounyan house as a change from the claustrophobic atmosphere of the dig. Later they met at the Paris Conference. Their actual meetings during the rest of their lives were few. It is sad that many of TE's letters were burnt together with a great deal of my parents' other correspondence during the dangerous time when Syria was under the Vichy government.

Ernest and Lawrence must have recognized in each other a certain similarity in the problems they had to deal with in life. Each found something valuable and necessary to complete their own complicated personalities. Both carried a millstone round the neck: for Lawrence his illegitimacy, for Ernest the fact that he was half Armenian, 'a mongrel' as he was constantly asserting. Perhaps the bastard and the mongrel felt they understood each other. Lawrence's father and mother had never married, had passed on their guilt at living in sin to their five stalwart boys, giving them life-long unease. 'Be kind to Ernest, he is not rigged for the open sea', Lawrence told mutual friends at Cambridge, perhaps a little patronizingly. Ernest did often see himself as a very small sailing boat at the mercy of every wind that blew. But he did have buoyancy tanks to keep him afloat through the worst storms, and he continued to struggle with whatever life brought him. He never thought for a moment of giving up, of withdrawing from the world – or changing his name. 'Talking to T.E. makes me feel like a well ironed handkerchief', he told Dora quaintly. The fact that his friend thought his latest outpouring of poetry ('Love's Trio') 'definitely worthwhile' kept him going through the black weeks when the Australian girl had disappeared for ever and was not answering letters. 'About once a week I have a wild impulse to burst my bonds,' he wrote to Lawrence, 'but I know that the results of leaving Aleppo would be worse than staying on.' After a while: 'Things are looking up in my soul. I am getting back into the conventional ways of thought and can even read the BMJ and give free play to bedside charm. I am not writing any more verse and trying to produce an atmosphere in which Dora can paint. Dancing has gone phut as I knew it would.' Ernest loved dancing but his sweating 'Groucho Marx' style was too energetic, and too unconventional to please most of his partners. Dora now refused to dance with him. She did not seem to need physical exercise as he did – desperately!

Just as the family at both ends of the Mediterranean were beginning to breathe again, to hope that one more crisis was past, and Ernest still on his feet, he wrote to Rickman:

> I have heard over the wireless that T.E. is lying in some bloody hospital in Dorset with his head stove in after a motorbike accident. Please will you find out whether he is alive or dead, maimed or whole. Let me know by letter. I am completely knocked silly by the thought that I may

never see him again . . . I shall die like a bloody rat in a poisoned run without anyone being aware of the stink . . . the past years of intimacy have been miraculous to me.

The next five days, while Lawrence lay unconscious, were unbearable for everyone. I wrote anxiously to John Rickman from Cambridge where I was 'swotting' for my School Certificate: 'I hope if the worst happens, we will be enough to make him think life still worth living' (I never actually met TE). When Lawrence died, Ernest, in his early fifties, faced the biggest and last volcanic eruption. His friends and relations could only peer through the smoke and flames, listen to the rumblings, and try to guess what was going on. He carried on operating, but was all the time struggling against an unbearable compulsion to write. He told me how he felt that 'TE' was compelling him to do so. In the long lonely evenings and the afternoons, he covered every available blank space on paperbacks, envelopes, prescription paper, margins of newspapers, with his illegible handwriting. His little secretary collected the scraps like any disciple anxiously trying to make sense of a master's words. He was sometimes very frightened. 'If for a moment I stop feeling or writing poetry,' he wrote to Rickman, 'I get the horrors and begin to smash up everything within reach.' 'Doggerel written by a mongrel' he called his writing in lighter moments:

> You never saw that crooked moon
> Behind Aleppo's citadel
> You never saw it shine again
> In Dorsetshire
> For you had died a week ago
> And I live on Aleppo wise
> To think our thoughts and gaieties.

The flow settled into conventional sonnet form and soon he had written 'a hundred and forty sonnets . . . I do long to see the effect of my ferment on another mind – stereoscopic effect, don't you know . . . Whether, as I careered along in the wind, I have been able to trail a sufficiency of streaming seaweed behind me to entangle the human mind has now to be determined. . . the struggle of a swimmer down a stretch of river . . . It is very hot, finances don't bear reflection and I am not seeing my kids for another nine months.'

His friends at Cambridge, who had been alarmed when the first 'book' ('Love's Trio') landed, were now, after comparing anxious notes, thankfully able to say that, in their opinion, 'the latest stuff is – *some of it* – very good indeed and should be published'. 'I have rung the bell under the very throne,' cried Ernest in triumph. Robin who, by that time, had had a stroke, wrote from his wheelchair that he had achieved a *real* poem. But the next long months of waiting were trying. After serious discussion, Ernest and Dora decided that, though the book's reception might upset him, it was a risk that they were prepared to take together. 'Dora', he wrote, 'so patient and so reticent, cannot but let out that there is considerable risk of my becoming famous after all these years. She has just painted five canvasses in twenty four hours including a couple of sunsets.' Ernest's grief was still sharp:

> I simply can't believe that I won't see him again. Some mornings, on waking, the realisation descends like a dish cover. I burst out swinging onto the empty floor in a wheeling waltz of thought which, if it produces verse, keeps me steady, but if not makes me very shaky. My difficulty is to balance between despair and exultation. My ability to write verse has left me very calm in daily life.

Even when Oxford University Press 'hurled it back without comment' and it seemed starkly apparent that 'now that T.E. is gone I shall never be understood by a living soul', he did not get too despondent. Another visit to England was due but, for once, he was rather dreading it. Things were going well in Aleppo: 'Operating first class. I like the people in so far as they are likeable.' 'Just back from a stunning weekend riding, sailing and painting. All three going on almost simultaneously. This morning Dora coped in mauve and blue with a storm while Brigit, with me as balast, and reefed down, sailed on, right over flooded lands and treacherous streams, until we were both exhausted, stepping out with the same relief and pride as one gets off a fresh horse.' But the children in boarding school were still unaccountably moaning and he was not looking forward to dealing with them. Once he set foot in England, every outline would be blurred by 'our unhappy young'. That summer they took a house by the river in Cambridge and my father stayed on in England longer than he should have, waiting for a publisher – 'doing a balancing act of my children against my father'.

But he had to go back with no decision made. The waiting continued: 'The moments drip by and no movement can remove one's bare head from the drip'. After the euphoria came another depression but not as bad as before: 'I am off in the deep again but this time the ship is better founded and not oversailed. I have very little poetry to show. I seem to achieve an incandescence but I have in my pocket a set of screens to interpose between each object contemplated and the source of illumination. I have better control.' Ernest often said that when he was in a poetic mood he saw eternity like a bright light, too dazzling to contemplate. In his late middle age, and with the help of what he called his 'full set of screens' (i.e., his conscious intelligence), he resisted the temptation to jump to any overpowering wave that would sweep him out to sea to blessed oblivion. He had more consideration for people round him, and most specially for Dora who had put up with so much. He wrote to John Rickman:

> I have caused her a hell of a lot of hell. She is a very present help in trouble, except at moments of her own submergences, which sometimes occur just as my own head is going under, perhaps for the third time. She is determined to work out her own salvation.

He looked back with regret to the times he had caused her sorrow and anxiety:

> When the wind dropped I was unable to shorten sail and start the motor which I know I should have done for her sake. I have visited some strange lands under full sail and full power. Now I have made myself stop writing verse, I have allowed the few remaining 'cat's paws' to scurry

across my lake unused and find myself in a hell of a temper trying to stow the sails without tearing them. I suppose I am still recognisably me and I have managed not to lose Dora.

Although he tried hard to sink into the medical world sometimes 'unvisited for months', and he succeeded to outward appearances, he could not quite prevent himself 'getting impatient when I think of my decaying body in contact with eternity and unable to fire off the fireworks lying in a schoolboy heap within'. Lecturing to the Aleppo Rotary Club on poetry – in French – did not quite satisfy his immortal longings.

Inevitably, when Cambridge University Press at last accepted his poetry, Ernest did not experience the expected apotheosis. Reviews were very scarce for *Ornament of Honour*. The *Palestine Post* hailed him as a 'Tennyson minor' and congratulated 'T.E.' on his private bard. The *Observer* said: 'Mr. Altounyan's remarkable poem will ensure that T.E. Lawrence will be immortalised. You can almost see the sun at Camelot,' but added, 'The fact that Altounyan wrote no poetry to the age of forty helps to explain why such burning intensity of vision is often marred by actual clumsiness, not only in the choice of words, but actually, in such elemental necessities of scansion and rhyme . . . his wings are weaker than his thought. All the same, the whole poem seems dictated from beyond the grave:

> My sorrow is a smooth and perfect thing
> Carved of silence that must now endure;
> No monument but a bewildering perfection
> Offered to a god obscure.
> Oh Sibyl seated by our springs of fate
> Thy perfect answers leave us passionate.

The last line needs no comment, no laurel. Merely to quote it is to be aware of poetry. It is as though Lawrence himself wrote this coloured fragment of autobiography with a smile upon his lips.' Some compared *Ornament of Honour* to *Adonais* or to *Lycidas*. 'Worthy,' they said, 'of the lasting anthologies of English poetry.' Certainly there were minnow-flashes of genius in almost all of the sonnets. Perhaps their sonnet form and their reminders of Shakespeare detracted from their originality, made them harder to appreciate.

Ernest was disappointed in the response to his book. He did not become 'famous', very few people wrote to him and hospital work remained the daily reality ('the unspeakable well-nigh unendurable contemplation of a train of slowly moving human beings for whom I can do nothing'). His tense, enthusiastic style alarmed the staid Alepines. The girls he liked to twirl madly about the dance floor thought him a little bit mad. Dora once more found she needed all her strength to counteract his depressions, which alternated with moods of destructiveness when he threatened to 'stamp a hole through my bottom boards and sing as I sink'. As he explained to John Rickman, 'the slit through which I see the enchanted garden is so narrow that I am past the aperture of vision almost at once. But the scenery within seems authentic.' If only he could have been sure of retaining the vision, in spite of all the utter boredom of everyday life.

But help was at hand. In the autumn of 1939 'every letter I write is overcast with the thought that by the time I am answered the war may be upon us'. 'Overcast'? Might he not have been secretly hoping that, before very long, he would be in uniform again?

Chapter Ten

Though we expected an instant wave of bombers – we were not sure what nationality – when we heard that war was declared on that hot September Sunday in 1939, nothing really happened for some months. I got my first job as chief clerk at the British Consulate in Aleppo, to replace the man who had gone back to England to join up. This made me feel important, though there was very little to do. I had left London the previous spring just before my twenty-first birthday. The sight of anemonies being sold in the streets usually brought on a wave of homesickness and this time I had given in. My training as a typist had just finished.

Susie was in Aleppo too, also considering what to do next, but she was set on going to France to help widowed Aunt Norah manage the Brittany manor house she was intending to run as a guest house. For the next seven years she was in a German internment camp in France; I kept that frozen image of her, waving to me from the ship in her red flowered dress.

When I was not typing at the Consulate, I was teaching English to two rather dull French officers. The effect on them when Paris fell in 1940 was like a balloon deflating. They left the next day and I was left wondering if they were Free or Vichy French.

If it had not been for his 'enigmatic' stepmother, Ernest would have felt guilty at rushing off at a day's notice, to Jerusalem to join up – as he did when there was a possibility that we in Syria would be interned by the Vichy French after the fall of Paris. The old man would probably have coped, even without his wife. He had weathered the horrors of 1914, nothing could be worse than that. Germans, Turks, French all looked the same when they were ill. While my father was away, the old magic held, patients kept on coming and the gold rolling in. 'Gives me the creeps,' was all his ungrateful son could say.

Ernest was forty-nine – 'fatter and greyer and generally sliding down hill', as he described himself. But Captain E.H.R. Altounyan, MC, RAMC, wrote at once to headquarters, offering his services. 'Besides his being eager to get into British uniform,' as Dora said, 'we did not like the idea of waking up in an enemy country and all being interned – or worse. It was rather awful leaving home in 1941, to do war work in Jerusalem. We assured the crowds of weeping patients and servants and nurses that we would come back.' 'I had just started making cherry jam in the sun', wrote Dora, so it must have been when the black cherries were ripe and the jam was on the roof in huge round pans which would take the summer months to cook. There were probably a few secretly glad of a respite from Ernest and his chivying.

Very soon he was strutting about very proud of the fact that he could still get his old Sam Browne belt into the same hole as in the last war when he was a young man in his twenties. The bulges above and below the waist did not matter. Keeping his stomach well in and his chin up – as he was always telling us to do – Ernest was very happy although he only got a pound a day and no money out of Syria. For some time he had very little to do as medical duty officer at one of the military hospitals in Jerusalem, sometimes sleeping in his old sleeping bag he had last used at the Somme. He took great pride in saluting the right people energetically, although his little finger, which had received a piece of shell in 1917 and which he had broken in a fall from his horse, stuck out against regulations. 'So far,' wrote Dora, 'he has only given one dose of cough mixture.' It seemed to them that 'dodderers and schoolboys' were the only ones considered fit for service, allowed 'to have a finger in the mud pie'. She wasn't desperately keen for him to go but, as in 1914, she knew that he would never be happy until he saw action. 'I believe it would be better for him if he can believe that he is in it.'

And very soon he was. His languages and his knowledge of

the country were too valuable to waste. Officially he was attached to the mosquito unit 'scouring Syria most of the time'. His car had a red elephant on it to show he was part of the Ninth Army, and he had an Arab Legion driver who was actually an Armenian. He became a colonel, 'only they don't wear scarlet tabs in this war'. Dora describes him as a 'sort of chameleon'. His medical 'cover' gave him freedom to roam the whole of the Middle East from the Turkish border to Egypt. His friends got used to him dropping in – usually most inconveniently – for breakfast, and his energy was unlimited. Dora wrote:

> He had been wandering about in the wildest parts of the Lebanon, high among villages where no one ever goes and the wildest sort of people live, riding and walking when the horse could go no further, 7000 feet or so high. There he met a man called Tyson from Coniston who was working in a lumber camp.

A month later:

> E is working all over the Alawite country from Lattakie to Tartous examining children's spleens ... he has been riding in the mountains for nine or ten hours camping at night without a tent, sleeping with his mosquito net hanging from a tree. Not bad for fifty four. He went there to find out what the people really think about their religion which is queer and a secret. They worship the moon among other things. A few years ago they started a new god. 'The almighty' is now living in enforced leisure in one of the best hotels in Damascus.

It was a pleasant change, as Dora said, after twenty-five years of solid surgery.

Black Grandpa was now about ninety. The news leaked out of Aleppo of how he had operated on his wife. A major abdominal operation of the most serious kind. 'And now she is getting better. I do hope my children have inherited some of the qualities of that amazing old man', said my mother.

Ernest did sometimes need to rush home to Jerusalem – to Dora. In spite of his mosquito net and his quinine, he did get a very serious bout of malaria. He had to be nursed during 'the most devastating heatwave – no ice, bottles in the windows swathed in towels trying to keep cool'.

After the Syrian Campaign of 1941, when the British and Free French took Syria from the Vichy French, Dora could sometimes go to Aleppo with him on 'flying visits'. His uniform kept him safe from being caught again in the hospital. He was 'under orders from headquarters', no time for anything but the most fleeting dip into family affairs. At Christmas he might or might not turn up – 'I have no idea where he is, probably on one or other bank of the Euphrates', said Dora. Bliss! Visits to Aleppo could, all the same, be harrowing for Ernest because of old friends who might be in prison for helping the enemy. Syria was full of every sort of spy for both sides as Aleppo was so near Turkey, which was neutral. Many of them were Armenians. He always did his best for them – 'Our house is now a sort of unofficial mess for anyone E comes across who is in need of a home'. One place Dora visited with Ernest in the course of his work was 'a happy little world of its own. Ninety five per cent of the inhabitants have malaria and it is a hotbed of political intrigue.'

Wherever he was Ernest always managed to turn up for their wedding anniversary:

> We celebrated twenty five years of marriage with twenty four hours 'home leave'. We picked ourselves a wedding bouquet of Dead Sea apples and other nightmare growths of this nightmare valley [Jericho] . . . I always think of that old raised map of Palestine Pater made, it seems funny to be sitting on the edge of it.

One year Dora had had all her teeth out and was hoping against hope that he would not come – 'what a hope . . . oh well . . .'

Though she was often worried about her scattered family, Dora found it very stimulating to be in Jerusalem ('most interesting and marvellous to be here'). Sometimes, it seemed we women would all have to be evacuated to South Africa. There was no news from Susie interned in France, or Titty making her perilous way back to London by boat, or Roger, about to become a fighter pilot. 'Oh heavens when will it end?' Dora wrote on 'airgraphs' to her sister Barbara.

Neither the eczema from which he had suffered since childhood, nor the asthma he was to develop after the war, interfered with Roger's career as a pilot. He became an instructor of instructors, much to my mother's relief. But she did not realize that, although he did not see active service, his AFC was awarded for his skill in teaching low flying at night in the Welsh valleys. One of the stories he allowed himself to tell was of knocking out a (French) pupil who had panicked and frozen to the controls.

I was happily independent on my own in Aleppo until I realized that being what they called 'locally recruited' I would be left behind if the Consulate had to pack up suddenly. This made me set out for Palestine too.

Jerusalem was for me as exciting as Ernest's first visit to the Lake District and Lanehead. It was a liberation and a widening of horizons. In Paris and London I had been lonely. Now I was part of a crowd of my contemporaries with apparently unlimited choice in making friends. Almost everyone was in uniform in a sort of disguise which added to the adventure. And the setting: to wake up morning after morning and find oneself still in Jerusalem, the holy city, was like living in paradise. The purity of the light and the air, the constant awareness that the ground itself was holy to no less than three religions, was thrilling even to an atheist like myself.

Journalism seemed to me then an attractive profession, so I got a job in the Public Information Office, a tall building in the middle of an olive grove. In the news room on the top floor we were constantly distracted in the evenings by the sun setting over the mountains of Moab. In spite of this, we worked hard at editing news items from England for the local press. If one of the papers used the very words we had invented as headlines we were happy. I did not get very far in my chosen profession because I married a journalist and, in time, had four children.

Dora's work in censorship used her love of languages to the full and gave her a lot of friends of her own and a life of her own – and she was earning her own money for once. The blackout was 'something fierce' and housekeeping trying because there was no variety in food. Rationing conditions in British mandate Palestine were very like those in England: very few vegetables – nothing but marrows and eggplants – no eggs, shopping tedious because every tube of paste or pot of jam purchased required an empty one handed in. 'This queer life of ours is like a dream. Or is Aleppo the dream?' My mother sometimes wished it had all happened twenty years sooner: 'I sometimes feel I have completely wasted the last twenty years, nothing to show except a family of children just ripe to be swept into the war'. She could be depressed at times just as Ernest could be; perhaps it only came upon her if she was alone. Perhaps she felt he was having a more interesting life. She had not quite forgotten the upset of the Australian girl of fifteen years ago. 'My hair is getting grey and I feel quite a hag sometimes' – (she was just under sixty). 'I wish my hair would go completely white, there are quite a lot of young women with white hair. I do envy the young with their unbounded energy.' Roger wrote describing his first solo flight. 'I'm sure that for him flying a plane is absolutely the height of bliss. The worst about getting old is not being able to do as much as I used to.'

But she still had enough time and energy to paint. She had an exhibition in Jerusalem on a day which turned out to be the hottest ever – 115 degrees – but 'quite a lot of people turned up in a nice steady stream on all the ten days it was on. Even though the local paper disappointingly only gave the number of pictures sold and no criticism, I made quite a nice little profit.' This would never have been possible in Aleppo where art meant copying postcards. While she was in Aleppo, Dora used to send pictures to the Lake Artists Exhibition. She wrote to her sister: 'If you need to fill up space, I should think you can use some of my old things. Change the titles and no one will notice. I've got one or two rather nice things here: a couple of Galilees which would look quite well among the Waste Waters, Grasmeres and Derwent Waters in the show. Oh well.' This was typical of my mother's assumed off-hand attitude to her painting which used to madden Ernest. In the same letter Dora mentioned that she had a sore arm from a typhoid injection, which put her off painting. It seems hardly credible that it was the first she had for seventeen years!

> Having successfully resisted the doctor's blandishments all that time I thought it silly to catch typhoid through my own cussedness, in wartime one is liable to much greater risks – so I let him stick the needle in my arm and he was astonished.

The last time Dora had considered it worth being innoculated for typhoid was when Brigit had nearly died of it as a baby.

Sometimes Jerusalem was difficult to live up to. Palm Sunday found Dora alone at home, washing her hair and cooking and tidying and doing odd jobs. 'A lot of people would give a fortune to be here this week ... perhaps I'll go out later and look at the crowds but from as far away as possible. I don't like crowds and they are apt to be something fierce at these times.' The old familiar debilitating yearning struck when least expected:

> I have been picking double jasmin but I would give anything for a pussy willow from the tree by the lake. . . . Lanehead as it used to be ... breakfast by a huge fire in the dining room: toast and eggs and marmalade ... things just coming out in the garden ... some snow still on the tops ... sometimes I wonder if I shall ever see Lanehead again. Gives me a pain.

On the other hand ... those 'long light cold wet evenings' ... would she ever again be able to live in England?

Jerusalem, the City of Light, kept up the blackout for several weeks after the rest of Palestine had abandoned it. But finally, on Christmas Eve 1945, Dora's patience was at an end: 'I shall jolly well light up every window'. Now, at last, everyone could go home.

Back at Lanehead on his last Army leave Ernest vowed, although not everyone quite believed him, that:

> After all these years I am longing to taste with the tip of my tongue peace and civilisation and ordinariness, and the devine dullness which we have forgotten ... Dora and I are cocooned in solitude of silky bliss. I'm ordering a whole cask of cider and I have wired to Ireland for a

servant. Dora has produced a ripping portrait of me. I have sailed to Peel Island and back for the first time in ten years. No one has congratulated me on my OBE so I continue to congratulate myself.

And in the New Year he at last became a Fellow of the Royal College of Surgeons: 'They have been and gone and done it, why I simply can't think. It is sad to have the honour when one has begun to wobble.' He was fifty-five. At his age his father had not even begun to build his hospital. But there would be enough reminders of this when he went back to Aleppo:

> Just about to replunge into the ME and before London quite fades, I'm dashing off a dozen 'bread and marge' as I fear that once again I may be cut off. But I feel very much on top of things phased for a last long spring determined that it shall be elegant and flashing. Life is ridiculously short, but does it matter if we realise that if it were a thousand years quality is the only thing to aim for.

After the war, Black Grandpa decided to make another trip to Europe. He was in his nineties and he and Peggy had not been West since the beginning of the war. His report of 'Our journey in August 1946 to Europe' begins:

> Now I should like to bring before you a picture of the small part which Mrs. Altounyan and I saw this last summer, of the result of the last world war. In every small thing every move we made we encountered unimaginable obstacles and difficulties.
>
> First the sailing date of the boat was changed three times. You know how this happened when our people left for Armenia. Then we were told we could only take small amounts of food stuff without permit. In Beirut we were told we needed a permit. To get this it was necessary to go to Damascus. On the boat there was no comfort. It was very crowded and disorderly.
>
> On arrival at Marseilles we wished to rest one night before taking the long train journey to Paris. This however was not possible as no rooms could be found in the hotels. So we took 1st class tickets to Paris. This did not assure us

seats in the train. Many people sat all night on their luggage in the corridors. We were very fortunate to be able to sit in a first class carriage. On reaching Paris there were no porters so we were obliged to get our luggage down from the train. Mrs. Altounyan put it down through the window of the train while I went down and caught it. There were no taxis so we walked to our hotel and a man carried the luggage.

The next day we spent in trying to reserve a seat in the train for London. This was not possible. Seats had been booked three weeks beforehand. So we went very very early to the station and found a porter to get us a seat.

At Calais we waited about three hours in a large crowd. Everyone carrying his own luggage. Cases knocking our legs in front other cases knocking our legs behind. Swiss 'jugging' our shoulders with their picks and their haversacks. At last we got on the channel boat. We were fortunate to get. As many were left behind until the next day. There was only one boat a day! and carried 1,400 passengers.

By this time we were hungry! and opened our tin of sandwiches. Hard black French bread (no butter) and fishpaste, but before we could eat it was announced that Passports would be examined by the English authorities so we joined the line and waited for our turn. At Dover we had to wait until almost everyone had landed before we could get back to our luggage.

On landing however we found quiet and order, a porter to carry our luggage, a policeman to direct us to our train, a beautiful clean and comfortably upholstered carriage and plenty of seats. Extra trains had been put on and dinner was served on the train.

In London we went at once to get our food ration tickets without these we could not obtain food. So we were able to buy just the same amount as the English people ... 70 grammes butter, 100 grammes sugar, 50 grammes tea. Each week you can have meat for one shilling and two pence (viz about 75 piastres Syrian). Milk 300 grammes each day. We got each one of us two eggs for the month!

Fish was not rationed, very cheap. Fruit and vegetables are not rationed. All things we could get with our tickets were much cheaper than in Aleppo. There is no black market in England, rich and poor are equal same food.

So many thousand houses have been destroyed by bombs many thousand people are homeless. We could not get a room in any hotel. We were very sorry to see London so wrecked and damaged. But all Londoners were going on quietly and patiently with their work. Trains buses and taxis are short but the people stand in long rows two by two waiting their turn. There was no grumbling or pushing. People chating [sic] and laughing with each other, just waiting. We also took our places in the line and waited for one hour for the train. It was the same for meals in restaurants waiting outside restaurants as soon as 2-3 comes out, 2-3 goes to the place that have come out to take their place. Every one is ready to help others that are in need of help.

From England we went to France. The conditions were very bad indeed. There were ration tickets but only those fortunate enough to pay the high prices of the black market could find white bread, butter, sugar.

In England and France the people look tired and strained. Children look pale and nervous, in Switzerland children look fat and rosy. People look happy and strong – carefree. Shops are full of cakes and sweets. Hotels are good and clean as in pre-war days with fine table linen. One is given large bath towels. In France and England paper on the tables and one has to carry one's own towels. In Switzerland trains are all electric and heated even small children give up their seats to elderly people. This is really the only place we were able to rest a little.

The people are interested in Armenians I was asked to speak over the radio about them answering questions about why so many of them are homeless.

On the way home in our French hotel we climbed many stairs to our hotel rooms very cold. Got only bad coffee and black rolls without butter for breakfast. Our voyage was very unpleasant. Small boat and very crowded and bad sea. So we were very glad to reach Beirut and more glad to reach Aleppo. We have to be thankful that the war did not come to Syria. It will take many more years for Europe to recover from this last horrible war.

When the telegram announcing his death in 1950 arrived in Barnes, it seemed as incredible to me, then in my middle thirties, as news of his marriage had been when I was a child. I told *The Times* he was ninety-nine. I could easily have said over a hundred. He was immortal! 'Was it a misprint or what?' asked my mother crossly. Her letter about the lying-in-state and the funeral reads like the burial of an elder statesman:

> All day streams of people of all sorts filed past and the coffin became embedded in wreaths. Two nurses kept watch day and night, lit by four tall candles borrowed from the Armenian Orthodox Church. The procession could hardly move for the crowds in the street, traffic stopped, church crammed, weeping Moslem women, all the Armenians you can think of and all the notables of the town. The coffin was carried by the usual ruffians in solemn gowns. Orations by a Moslem doctor, an Armenian bishop, an American missionary, a protestant pastor. Nurses singing. The low sun came through the window and lit up the wreaths. It was nearly dusk when the coffin was put in a grave in the church enclosure.

The burial was to have been in the hospital garden but the government refused permission at the last moment. Then there was endless trouble about the exact height of the monument Dora was designing. The Church elders insisted that it should not be more than ten inches above the ground in order not to attract attention! Ernest, very angry, said that if they persisted he would bury his father elsewhere – the American Boys' College up on the hill would be proud to have him. The Armenian Protestant Church which, as everyone knew, was built with money donated by The Big Doctor in memory of his first wife, has hardly any land round it, no space for even one grave. It is hardly surprising that the caretaker's wife is from time to time tempted to hang her washing so that it drips onto

The Unknown Remembered Gate

Black Grandpa's stone under the church wall, scandalizing passing friends or relatives on a flying visit to Aleppo. Aunt Norah died in the same year as her father and was also buried in Aleppo.

Even before the statutory forty days of mourning for Black Grandpa were over, Aleppo was shaken by rumours that 'the widow' was being turned out of her home, had nowhere to go. Before 'She' left, Ernest and Norah had sessions with 'Her' every evening going over cupboards full of papers. The safe was ceremoniously opened in the presence of government officials and found to be empty. 'Fresh evidence of rapacity and the results of revenge were constantly turned up, attempts to sell property that wasn't hers, no sign of the 20,000 gold pounds which all Aleppo knew was in a bank in Switzerland – and so on.' My father describes the last scene – which he could not help finding 'very amusing': 'During the last inspection and handing over of the premises, I fell down a six foot pit and cut my wrist and bruised my scaphoid [wrist] so badly that I can no longer operate.' The constant nightmare.

It was to be thirty years before I met 'Her' again. After she had left Aleppo she no longer existed for us – not for about twenty years anyway. Then, as I researched into my grandfather's life, she started to haunt me as if asking to come back – to state her case as it were. In the late seventies I wrote a very tentative note to an address in Beirut where she had made her home since leaving Aleppo. It was like throwing a bottle message into the waves. With unnerving speed a blue envelope came back – the kind of blue my mother always used for her letters to us. Her address was still Farnham where her father had been a farmer – a 'contaminated area' for us by association with her. The writing was spidery but that was not surprising, considering she was at least eighty. But there was no mistaking the warmth of the letter: 'I am in Farnham for a bit. Come and see me.'

The faded green door of the little cottage had a notice on it: 'Bang very hard and push the door if I don't answer'. But I hardly had time to touch the knocker before the door was opened from the inside, as they say in fairy-tales. And there 'She' was. Tall, dignified, much more stylish than I remembered. 'This is an occasion', I heard myself say. And she, in the same formal way, 'This is indeed'. And we kissed carefully for perhaps the first time in our lives. The Altounyans were never given to kissing.

Remembering my grandfather's sumptuous drawing-room, the cottage which her sister had given her 'in case Beirut when wrong' and she was forced to leave suddenly, did not suit her at all. It looked more like a second-hand furniture shop to me. There was a fierce gas fire and a lot of crocheted wool in an uncomfortable-looking chair.

We sipped tea, getting over the first shock, each of us replacing our minds' faded image with a new one. We had last met when I was under thirty and just married, and she was in her middle forties. Her skin was like her hair, very good for eighty, and she had the same shy smile and soft, rather whiny voice we used to find so irritating.

She did not want to speak about Beirut, but she told me that, when the fighting started, she had been rescued from her big house on the frontline and taken to the Armenian monastery of Antelias. There she had lived for some months – but she soon had to return to protect her house from refugees. It often came under shell fire.

> Such a noise. I had not time to move or think between the blasts. Often I was alone in the whole building because the nuns on the top floor, and everyone else, had run away. They were frightened. When the guns were in the street below I went into the kitchen because it was at the back, and I had two walls to protect me though I do know now that shells come through double walls. At every blast the glass fell out of my windows, and then the curtains fell, a tangled heap of curtains and plaster and glass on the floor! In the middle of the night it was always light outside because of all the burning cars. In any lull I made myself another cup of tea . . . But, please, I don't want to talk about Beirut.

Many of the legends about my grandfather I already knew, of course, but she could add tiny details that lit up the 'pebbles' from a new angle. I hoped for new facts he might have told her about his mother, left alone in Sivas. But there was only, 'She could roll out twenty-nine sheets of baklava pastry from one small roll of dough'. 'Your grandfather loved dining on the terrace in the summer, but if it got later than nine o'clock, I would threaten moving downstairs and, you know, he would be over like a flash'. I remembered sadly how my mother would often wait till midnight for my father to finish surgery, nodding off to sleep now and then but *never* protesting. And when he did come he seemed too tired to eat. 'I loved your father', she said more than once. That was a surprise but, after all, they were the same generation:

> Sometimes he would come in, very late in the afternoon, exhausted, with the excuse of asking how the old man was. I knew they had been together all the morning. I guessed that he dreaded going home so late – your mother would be lying down for her afternoon siesta, no one in your kitchen. So I would rouse my cook. He always ate with such an appetite in our house.

Could one believe anything she said? As we got to know each other better I dared ask her 'How on earth . . .?' Yes, she admitted, fifty years was a huge gap. But then she took out 'snaps' of their honeymoon: bathing parties, riding, picnics by the lake, boating and grand balls at the Union Française in Aleppo, which she enjoyed a lot more than my mother ever did. The old doctor looked so young and handsome in white tie and tails, enjoying everything so much.

I had to ask her about the famous operation during the Second World War. 'There was no one else I could trust', she said. And him ninety.

> The Australian doctor had opened me up and said 'hopeless. We might as well give up.' But your grandfather told me later that he first had to forget the fact that I was his wife and only think firmly 'the patient must survive'. I call tell you he nearly died himself. When I at last opened my eyes and looked at him his face was ashen. I must get well for his sake, I said.

Besides memories, which she carefully listed in pencil when

she was going to see me, she brought me things, sometimes quite heavy things, even when she had had to be wheeled in a chair across the shattered airport at Beirut. She brought a very heavy, leather-bound complete Shakespeare my grandfather had won as a *second* prize 'for Declamation at the Central Turkey College. Aintab July 1880.' That book had come from New York to Aintab in the last century, some of the way on mule-back. Then it was carried again on mule-back when the newly married Assadour and Harriet set out for a medical tour of the villages on the way to Aleppo. I doubt if he had ever looked into it. She also brought me his attaché case pasted all over with labels: Cunard White Star Line Stateroom Baggage, date 1939. That must have been the time he went to New York for his honorary degree. There were torn labels on which one could just read the names of famous hotels in Paris, Rome, Florence ... She brought me his travelling inkpots for black and red ink, non-spill for writing prescriptions in the saddle. She brought me what was probably the first thermometer Aleppo had ever seen.

And there were many photographs, some of which I knew well, like the large sepia one of herself: 'the 1930s sports girl' posed on a hill against the sunset, with Aleppo Castle in the background, hair blowing, body straining back against two fine dogs on a leash. This flattering picture had been in the local photographer's window for us to scoff at as we passed. 'I think I'll keep that one a little longer', she said.

As I talked to her I thought of the great difference between her and my mother and what a pity that differences of class had kept them apart. Though Dora had been kindness itself to her Armenian servants, the fact that 'She' was 'not a lady' was an insurmountable barrier.

Chapter Eleven

ERNEST DID not find his return to Aleppo after the war as trying as he had expected. This was partly because Black Grandpa had, by then, almost completely given up operating: 'He was no longer safe . . . his hand was quite steady and he got away with major ops but his judgement failed sometimes and you never knew what impossibility he might comtemplate.' This meant an enormous increase in self-confidence in Ernest even though he found returning to surgery after a gap of seven years tremendously hard.

> What wears me out is this immense variety of work which never allows one to become skilled . . . I realise, with a pang, that I have only six more years left in which to do all that I want to do in the way of surgery. I intend to tackle the latest operation for deafness and, of course, operate on the heart and lung. I am doing the new op on the prostate which is a winner . . . if all goes well the patient is up and dry in six days . . . I am an extremely competent surgeon and will be able to keep the place going until Roger comes. I've celebrated the FRCS by doing the first thymectomy outside the USA and UK, and am now steering towards brain surgery and lungs. That will clear up the whole of the poor old boxy except eyes, which I cannot bear to tackle, and midwifery, which my physique simply won't stand for . . . the only thing I am any good at is to do small simple things that are dangerous and require short bouts of intense concentration. I have not yet succeeded in running at a smooth

> cruising speed that is noiseless and economical and harmless to my surroundings. I find it at the moment impossible to imagine that I was ever a soldier or poet. Yes, writing poetry is dangerous for one risks complete sanity.

A 'smooth cruising speed' was not his style and never would be. That was the fundamental difference between Ernest and his father. A small sailing boat hardly ever manages a steady progress through the water. Black Grandpa's progress was as purring and steady as his favourite Voisin car, or his best horse. And Ernest needed drama like a boat needs a breeze. The next ten years were to be stormy enough even for him. If there was no wind he would always manage to raise some!

At the first nurses' graduation ceremony after his father's death, Ernest was firmly in control:

> I am very pleased to welcome you all here this afternoon, for everyone in this room is either a friend of the hospital or the relative of someone working with us. As friends therefore and without formality, let us spend an hour together recalling the past and looking forward to the future. It is almost exactly forty three years since I made my first speech as a trembling schoolboy. Although it is now thirty two years since my wife and I settled to work among you, this is the first time I feel quite grown up. At the last graduation three years ago, my Father was still here and of course to my Father I always seemed young and foolish, though quite amiable. It is also the last time I shall feel really grown up, for next year my son will be beginning and to a son a father, however amiable, is certainly very old and not a little foolish.

That year, nine nurses graduated, which was a record. Here my father was at his most staid and charming. Most of the fireworks were left out because, after all, many of the audience did not understand English very well. He apologized to the graduates for calling them 'little donkeys' – 'this is not my real opinion' – he apologized to the patients if 'this nursing of ours that I have been talking about is not much after all. Please remember that we are almost a hundred years behind the rest of the world.' But, fearing to offend some of the Syrian dignitaries present: 'Syria is a brand new country . . . I hope, in fact I am sure, that in the next few years hospitals will be organised each with their medical schools and the medicine and the surgery of Syria will take its place proudly with the medicine and surgery of the rest of the world.' So far so good. The family listened with drawn breath. Ernest had decided to behave himself for once.

For the next few years things went 'hummingly', to use one of his favourite expressions. He had a new project to keep him occupied. 'Last night I decided to spend my gold reserve in building on a private wing to the hospital. No one knows the risk I am running better than I do, but I must make a bid for the rich snobs of this town.' This desperate last-ditch attitude was toned down by Roger and his sisters. 'I haven't a bean,' Ernest would bluster, 'my stepmother having gone off with all the spare cash', but Brigit and Roger planned and launched an appeal and went into facts and figures. The hospital was to be second to none in the Middle East, with the nurses' training school for Armenian girls a means of helping Arab (and Armenian) refugees. The results were disappointing though. One trusty friend actually sent a cheque for £3: 'You really must come and see us. Unfortunately my wife and I are just leaving for a world trip.' And much more to the same effect. Some were scolding: 'You must drop all that nonsense about it being unpleasant to beg for money. You have devoted your life and your fortune to a good cause and if it has been worthwhile it is worthwhile arousing sufficient interest in England to ensure the good work is carried on.' Another wrote: 'Your hospital sounds too much for one man to carry on single handed. I suppose you can get government aid if you surrender a measure of control – which you are too individualistic to do.' The 'penniless' project went ahead 'by leaps and bounds'. 'The lift, that hallmark of oriental modernity, is on the high seas.' Selling land was always the last resort but, as Brigit wrote, 'owing to the inefficiency of the local government our land has not yet been surveyed, or something – there are people willing to buy land but we cannot get the money' – because of complicated inheritance laws.

Everyone was glad Black Grandpa was not there to see the fifty-year-old roof coming off to build the new storey on top.

Some of the beams had been reduced to filigree work by rust. It was a miracle it had not fallen long ago. We had to take down every beam, whether sound or not, as a precaution. The old hospital was filled with rubble and and looked like a newly bombed house.

The Aleppo masons had not lost their old skills and Brigit found it 'great fun' to see them shape and place their stones. The new wing was of the same primrose-coloured stone as the rest of the building. Ernest was afraid it would turn out 'a folly' – Aleppo was full of half-built palaces left to public ridicule when the cash ran out – but he boasted about the separate food lift to the kitchen as well as the big one 'set up by a cockney engineer'. The private wards painted in every shade of pastel were 'lit by a system of internal lighting which is a dream'. 'If it all tumbles down on top of us next month for want of cash, I shall still think it worthwhile having attempted.' The roof did not fall in.

All the time the building was going on, the work of the hospital went on too. Ernest 'never missed an op', the hospital kept full all the time: 'I simply don't know how those builders do the work without letting us down a single day either for water or electricity'.

Roger, in the middle of his midwifery course ('Baby count stands at nine – all screaming') received and sent instructions almost daily about the hospital and the new building. Then two shock waves reach Aleppo. Roger failed his finals the first time, although he succeeded a few months later. And he announced he was to marry a German girl, Hella Schumacher. 'Think of everything you can imagine Daddy saying – and then double it. But he really doesn't mean it.' Dora was pleased. After all, her grandmother had been German Swiss and she loved speaking the language.

Roger and his fresh and blooming bride, dressed all in pink, arrived just in time to open the new wing. But though Ernest and Roger worked as hard as usual, somehow the private patients did not arrive and most of the lovely rooms remained empty. 'Somehow I don't go down with the rich', wrote Ernest.

I shall plod on, but require a streak of real luck such as a successful case with a well known man. So far my well known men have turned up their toes and died with monotonous unanimity. I am up against my war record and fee splitting and strong French competition. If I had no son I would chuck it at once. . . . Roger is working his head off and I only hope he won't feel as bitter as I do about working in a strange land. I warned him about the pitfalls of working among strangers and he would not listen. I am quite prepared to close down and let him begin again elsewhere.

Roger did not consider he was working among strangers. He had been born in Aleppo. Without his father continually undermining his authority he would probably have got on quite well. Ernest's suspicion of the Oriental mind – 'always suspecting some catch, and becoming angry if he cannot find it' – was not Roger's. He expected to work on friendly terms with everyone, whatever their nationality. He did not understand Ernest's inverted snobbery which drove him to be so rude to the very people on whom the hospital depended – the rich upper class of Aleppo. Ernest's peculiar brand of cussedness, which made him bite the hand which would have fed him, seemed to come from left-over adolescence. It need not have been true that 'people just refuse to consider a worthy man being succeeded by a respectable son'.

As usual when Ernest felt defeated he piled on the negatives: he had worked for thirty years and accomplished nothing – *nothing*. Everything had always gone wrong. The only thing he knew he could do was write poetry. Of course, he knew that this was nonsense. Now that Roger was there he could have left but he could not allow himself to see that his son would probably get on much better without him. With his father gone, he was now faced each day with patients saying how like his grandfather his son Roger was – *Inshallah* he would be as good. As Roger became popular, especially with the younger generation, without apparently lifting a finger, Ernest, against his better nature, could not help bullying him in every subtle way he could. Very soon Roger was having his own form of nervous breakdown. It was obvious that one of them had to go. Roger already had two children and, it was subsequently discovered, was about to be the father of twins. In his own words:

> After the war, qualifying in medicine by the skin of my teeth, I had to go back to Aleppo . . . There I practised medicine and surgery under heroic do-it-yourself conditions not in the Belgian Congo but in the Middle East. For five frantic years I attempted to cope with tuberculosis, typhoid, tetanus and trauma of all kinds. Until local zenophobia became too hot for me and I returned to England depressed and disillusioned.

He left Aleppo in 1954.

As he was recovering from the nervous breakdown, a research laboratory provided him with his first hope, and gradually he found himself immersed in what, at serious moments, he would call 'the tragedy of chronic chest disease'.

> When I was a child allergic disease was an even greater mystery than it is today. It is hardly surprising that I was given no help by the medical profession in the early twenties. My eczema was not life threatening but it caused me years of anguish: the frequent bouts of itching were followed by the flowing of blood and tears . . . I was taken by my father to see specialists in London. They all agreed that I had eczema but treatments varied widely. One advised that I should stop eating chocolate, probably because I had admitted to a passion for it – another ordered that I have no baths – this suited me fine. Medical baths hurt like hell. . . . But I continued to have eczema just the same . . . and when everything had failed it began to be suggested that it was my fault.

The first attack of asthma came, not surprisingly, after the war when he was under pressure to take his finals as soon as possible and join his father and grandfather in Aleppo:

One night I awoke fighting for breath and thought I was about to die. The next morning the memory was so blurred and so unreal that I convinced myself that it had been a nightmare – especially as I now felt reasonably well – but the same thing occurred the following night.

Again, when everything failed, he was told by the doctor who suddenly turned into 'a funny ha ha medical sergeant major, "it is quite all right my lad you have ONLY got asthma. The old psyche you know ... don't worry about yourself so much."' After this sort of treatment Roger must have seen what his life work was to be. He described himself as an asthmatic who also happened to be a doctor. 'An asthmatic is rather a proud fellow who secretly believes himself to be independent and self reliant. Unfortunately he is not that since he has to live out his life in a leaky fragile boat – somewhere out there in the bay.' The doctor's duty was to be the 'coast-guard', to keep watch and to give help the moment it was needed. 'Only the man in the boat knows whether the water is rising or falling.' Roger was in a unique position: both on shore and in the boat. Roger's advice to doctors dealing with patients – especially asthma patients – was to act as if you had all the time in the world. And he carried this out in his daily life sometimes to the annoyance of those closest to him. He had that child's capacity for getting absorbed in play especially if it involved anything to do with wind or water. I can see him now coming gently down the lake before the wind, in our old boat *Mavis* with the dark brown sail well out, looking like a blousy overloaded barge. Roger is completely relaxed at the helm, steering with a knee over the tiller, keeping his pipe alight with one hand, the other perhaps disentangling a fishing line or rescuing something just dropped overboard by a child. The boat is full of children of all ages, not a life-jacket between them, most of them doing things which 'Ukartha' would not approve of: trailing hands, feet, even hair in the water, leaning out dangerously and *never*, if they could help it, obeying orders. Roger himself took to the water when very young. There is an old picture of him at hardly more than six months old sitting up fatly grinning in a wicker cradle wedged between the thwarts of the Collingwoods' old boat –

another *Swallow*. And that song he was so fond of: 'Take my money take my coat leave me with my fishing boat . . .'.

Perhaps to tease his eldest sister, Roger often insisted to me that he was not an intellectual – anything but that. I'm afraid we never let him forget the time he came back from school proudly announcing that he had read 'a book', it was a healthy reaction for a boy who had two such contrasting grandfathers: Black Grandpa who was never known to read anything but medical books, and White Grandpa who not only read books – for pleasure – but wrote them too. His mother and her siblings were brought up by their father to have 'an adult attitude towards learning'. His uncle Robin only went to Rugby when he was thirteen, being educated at home till then. This was all very well in the careful atmosphere of Lanehead but could get diluted by the different setting of Aleppo. Added to this, his father's constant boast that he was a better poet than a doctor, though not at all true must have firmed his son's resolve not to get in such a muddle himself. He only just managed to qualify as a doctor with the very poorest of degrees and he had no basic training as a scientist but that did not prevent him devoting himself heart and soul to original research once he had decided what his work was to be.

During the fifteen odd years during which Roger and a team of scientists worked on the discovery which was eventually to be called 'Intal', every sort of set-back either occurred naturally or was put in their way. In the very early days there was so much official opposition and pessimism that, more than once, the team was ordered to stop work 'forthwith'. Roger himself was dismissed and even threatened. As he said, they soon became adept at 'avoiding any sort of limelight' and learned to 'exhibit practically no profile, hoping that they would be forgotten and allowed to work on unobserved. Over their heads, managements changed and takeovers happened. There was a certain amount of what he called 'unplanned good fortune' and a great deal of 'being messed about'.

When the wheel of fortune took yet another turn, suddenly, the team found itself back in favour for good, actually receiving encouragement and funds. A tidy ten years after he left Syria, Roger was able to write 'Eureka'. On 19 January 1965, disodium cromoglycate (later to be called Intal) was discovered. However, the compound was found to be very effective if inhaled but useless if taken by mouth. 'So naturally I thought of my years in the RAF sitting behind a propeller. Why not get asthmatics to inhale through a tube inside which a propeller rotates and releases the drug.' The trouble was that if the propeller rotated evenly the drug was not directed down the lungs. After more months of trial and error, with an engineer friend and himself working on an apparatus set up on the arm of a sitting-room chair, the 'spinhaler' ('I thought of the name in my bath') was invented.

Roger kept very quiet on the subject of his work through all those years. Now and then, he would say that perhaps he was discovering something which would be as famous as penicillin. He never told us that all his experiments were carried out on his own lungs 'because you can't induce asthma in rats'. After his death, there were his laboratory notes, pages and pages of his terrible childish writing, more than three thousand experiments carried out during his clinics. The patients would be given 'the latest' – if it was safe. When it was all over, we did hear of a few 'amusing incidents' of the many which might have cost him his life and probably did progressive harm to his lungs. Here is just one: they began this time to inject with confidence since they had been trying it on monkeys for months. But very soon they had to stop as their patient was feeling a burning sensation 'just like being dipped fairly painlessly in boiling oil' and he turned bright red and all his hairs started to stand on end. Fortunately, that was not one of the times when an ambulance had to be called – urgently.

As soon as he realized that Roger was not coming back, Ernest 'changed tack':

> Whether I find the money coming in or not I shall be carrying on. I am daily more and more convinced that we are more and more necessary in this country (in spite of what Roger says) and I feel quite capable of directing this show for another ten years – if I can get a set of youngsters to *bully* and cajole ...
>
> Publicity is my slogan at the moment. It may make just

the difference in my getting an endowment for my medical centre based on the hospital which I am planning ... Everything is going so wrong with us that there must be a change for the better ... of course I may fail, and then, of course, Roger will have the laugh of me. But you can count on me going down with the flag nailed to some part of my anatomy.

In 1956 Britain, France and Israel invaded Egypt to prevent the Suez Canal being blocked. They were stopped by the intervention of the United Nations and America. The canal was reopened in 1957 but the position of the Altounyans in Aleppo went from bad to worse from then on.

The new building stood up well. The end came in a more unexpected way. My parents were in England, celebrating – cautiously – because they had at last received an offer of a little money, when the Suez affair happened. Ernest refused to accept that he would never be allowed to go back. He refused to sell out. All advice to do so made him more determined to hang on. He declared that he still had work to do in Syria. To help the 'cash flow' he managed to get what he called 'a bottle washer's job' as temporary registrar in a hospital on the Isle of Man. Curiously, he and Dora felt even more cut off there than they sometimes did in Syria.

> This curious dead-end place hermetically sealed off. That little bit of sea makes us feel cut off from the world. We are comfortable here and it is fairly cheap. People are very kind. The only snag is that Ernest is bored.

It was hard to imagine him playing Father Christmas at the hospital. At Christmas 1957 they sent out three hundred cards – little cries fluttering all over the world. From Aleppo came a constant stream of letters in many languages telling of the blackest betrayals. When Ernest's contract ended they were temporarily barred even from Lanehead because it was let to a curious religious sect who 'expect the second coming rather soon and want to stay till the end of July'. Not surprisingly, Dora had a stroke. For the rest of her life her right painting arm was stiff and almost unusable. That was the end of her beautifully written letters. But she tapped away on the typewriter and patiently worked at her paralysed hand until she was again able to dress herself. She even began to paint again with her left hand.

Ernest went on being bullishly determined to go back to Aleppo – because it was impossible. They were, sadistically, given a tourist visa in 1959. My mother's letters continued calmy from Aleppo as if there had been no change:

> Everybody is friendly (and I mean everybody). We are greeted like long lost relations by people of every community and every class. It has really been quite touching. The spate of visitors has abated now and the bunches and baskets of flowers, but for the first ten days they were overwhelming . . . we still do not know if we are staying or not, but the indications seem favourable. The cemetery is built over but not so that I cannot see the citadel for which I am very thankful. We found three years' accumulation of mail waiting for us . . . some letters which really ought to have been sent on. But there is nothing to be done about it now.

But gradually, the nightmare atmosphere began to pervade even my mother's letters which tried so hard to be cheerful:

> The chief feature of the landscape is now an enormous advertisement: a 'Tide' packet, complete with housewife, and a pile of washing, twenty feet across. By the mercy of heaven it does not hide the citadel . . . This is not the place to tell the sad story of our ex-chauffeur. We were very fond of him, you know, and it has been rather a shock to hear how thoroughly swindled we have been by him. Aleppo is awfully noisy. Cars hoot unrestrainedly and continually. The normal street cries like the khake sellers, the mulberry sellers, the man who tinkles the cups for iced drinks, are all drowned in the shattering din of cars. There is only one hour between two and three in the morning when it is quiet. We have a wireless but don't seem to be able to get it to say anything . . . Everything is horribly complicated. Who is to be trusted?

Ernest was waiting for permission to resume his work. He noted modern improvements in this New Syria: the excellent roads, fields well ploughed by the latest in tractors, and many villages with electricity from 'natty little pumping stations'. A great new dam was being constructed on the Euphrates and, at last, there was a huge petrol refinery at Homs. But it seemed to him that:

> An orderly terror reigned. The governor was a man of thirty six seldom mentioned by name and his instrument was an absolutely disciplined secret police, instantly noticeable by their dour uneasy bearing and obvious sinister loyalty to someone. For the first time in all my years in Syria I noticed the sudden frightened silence that fell, in the middle of a conversation, when a servant or even a small child, entered the room. This chilled me more than the tapping of the telephones, the car that patiently followed me wherever I went, or the men in the hired window, across the road from our house, who patiently noted down our visitors ... and yet people came and invited us for meals and this is what decided me to stay if I somehow could.

The flowers, the crowds on the station platform, the party invitations had been too much for the impatient young men building the new Syria, or what my father called 'a modern fascist Arab state'. Ernest and Dora were still hoping to be allowed to stay when, in 1959, about a hundred years after Black Grandpa's birth in Sivas, they 'were expelled suddenly, unexpectedly, on three days notice by an order presented by a corporal. Nor did the Colonel Gauleiter consent to see [me] or vouchsafe the smallest explanation. A somewhat superior thug in a very superior car saw us off in complete silence onto the plane. Time 6.30 a.m.'

Hardly had my parents left when our solid fortress house was knocked down by efficient modern bulldozers. Only a generation before it had been built by human hands, chipping stone, planing wood and digging foundations. Tons of cement had been mixed by hand, carried up rickety wooden ladders and slapped on walls and roofs. An army of men had dug cisterns and wells. Brass and copper fittings for the doors had come all the way from England. The best craftsmen in Aleppo had mixed the paint for the woodwork, taken a pride in each glossy door as if it was a work of art. Everything had been built to last. But we had omitted one thing: to sacrifice a cock on the foundations. So Aleppo had not been surprised when the baby got typhoid the year we moved in and the doctor fell off his horse, breaking both wrists and both legs. Perhaps Armenians, comparative newcomers like the Altounyans, should have sacrificed *two* cocks. A few short months after my parents had been turned out of the country there was not even a hole in the ground to show where their house had been – only a great modern cinema called 'Ugarit'. And the name of the street between the house and the hospital was no longer Sharia Altounyan.

The hospital was turned into a school and immediately lost its immaculately self-sufficient, compact air behind the ragged nationalist banners draped across the balconies. Grandpa's ghost may still be wandering round the wards, though he was never a one for living in the past.

Back at Lanehead for good, Ernest and Dora swept the cobwebs of decades from behind the pictures. Ernest's new 'tack' was to be a 'remittance man', living on cheques from Aleppo, his 'surgeon's hand blackened and coarsened with coke and logs'. Between cheques he pretended he was living on what he got from writing talks for the BBC – 'I'm no longer proud and don't mind how much my work is mauled as long as I can pay for the coal'. When the long-awaited packing cases arrived by sea from Aleppo they were mostly filled with rubbish, things my mother did not particularly value: hideous embroideries of Queen Zenobia done in silk and scratchy sequins, or the second-best samovar, not the brass one she used every day for afternoon tea in the drawing-room, nor her own Georgian teapot. That arrived months later, buried in a parcel of pistachio nuts.

Ernest found a new formula: he explained to everyone that he was selling up in order to try and defeat death duties 'and be able to leave you all something'. He very much doubted that the grandchildren, 'immensely Welfare and destructive', would allow him to live the necessary five years. He was fond of them in his way, although he hated being called 'Grandpa'. He told them that he was glad they were homesick for Syria *now*, and were not reserving it for their old age. They could not understand why a dropped toffee-paper set him off in a diatribe against the Labour Government. My father equated Labour with sloppiness in everything. As a doctor, he did not approve of the National Health Service for the usual Tory reasons. He was always ready to point out how Labour Britain was unable to understand a hard-working nonsocialist person like him. He pretended not to mind being short of money but he was not used to skimping and was touchy about being considered poor. He really had not the smallest idea of what money in England meant since he had always lived like royalty in Aleppo. For instance, the house my family and I lived in at the time cost three thousand and something pounds. When he came to visit us he could not understand, first that we had a mortgage, and then that the tiny box of a house really cost so much.

Fortunately for everyone, his energies were taken up lecturing: to Chatham House, the BBC, St Antony's Oxford, Jesus College Cambridge, Grasmere United Nations Society and, when there was time, Women's Institutes. He was a rich mine for arrangers of talks and, although his less sophisticated audiences must sometimes have been puzzled and overwhelmed by the sheer force of language, they usually ended by being stimulated – if not stunned! He told the BBC:

> Seventy years ago my Scottish Irish mother from Armagh and my Armenian father from a town not so far from the Caucasus produced a very mongrel boy. I have always maintained that this mixture gave me quite a useful stereoscopic view of East and West . . . Of these seventy years thirty were lived in the United Kingdom and forty in the Middle East, mostly in Aleppo, a city now the size of Belfast and just as lively.

(The fact that he was a 'mongrel' comes into almost all his speeches.)

To Chatham House he tried to explain 'the theme whose evolution was to blow so much of Western influence sky high in

1956. . . . Indeed the bits of that explosion are still falling about our persons.' Ernest thought that the Mandate plan, which gave some of the Middle Eastern countries to the care of Britain and France for twenty-five years, prolonged the adolescence of the Arab because 'it did not teach the rudiments of self-government . . . There is no way of growing up but the hard way.' We had, overnight, changed our attitude from a friendly, caring uncle to a cold and distant acquaintance. However much the Arabs had been clamouring for independence they had no wish to cut off personal contact. They still needed us to advise and guide. That 'rather unpleasant Eastern variety of Teddy Boy', who had turned him out of Syria so roughly, would not have happened if we had at least tried to meet the Arabs on equal terms as friends:

> At the end of the second world war, when we had secured the complete cessation of the mandate, bundled off the angry French, set them up with President and Prime Minister and removed – before their unbelieving eyes – every soldier we had got – we returned with an ambassador who was instructed not to have more to do with them than was strictly necessary . . . he had been chosen because he had never served in the Middle East and disliked wogs in general.
>
> At Suez there was a moment [Ernest was convinced] when we could have laughed even that one off . . . Nasser never dreamed at his wildest that he would ever get away with it . . . he would have been extremely pleased (when the deed was done) to see someone from London to advise him in the friendliest manner but alas . . . we went all 'protocolaire' . . . What do any of us really want in life? Law and order? I wonder. I believe that each of us, black, brown, yellow, or pinky white, wants adventure and to be somehow the hero of it. We only want just enough law-and-order to serve as an island base for those adventures. The Middle Easterner up to 1914 for various reasons did not have that 'just enough' and the words England, America, France, rang in his ear like a magic chime. By the end of the *first* war he had learned the trick. He found

out that Westerners were not demi-gods. A little sad but glad, he held out his hand to his miraculously favoured equals – and he was rejected ...

This was a dangerous attitude for the West to take towards such sturdy individuals as the multi-racial inhabitants of the Middle East. They have been reacting strongly ever since.

Perhaps it was not as simple as that. The world had got more complicated than he knew. He could not have guessed the full effect oil would have on every aspect of Middle Eastern life. He believed in his 'little prescription', which T.E. Lawrence ('the most important single impact in my life') had passed on to him:

> Each unit of living matter can only maintain valuable contact with another unit of matter on the assumption that one equals one. If you are to co-habit the same unit of space you must weigh the same and set about co-functioning.

Ernest sometimes got restless – and bored. He would go off in his van on a round of visits to friends living round the lake, turning up at mealtimes, preferably breakfast. Every day he took Dora out for a drive. Sometimes he managed to get so high up the Old Man that the van was almost standing on its end, but Dora could look at the view and, after all, that is what they had been promising themselves through all those years of hell.

And there was 'The Book'. Somehow, what with one thing and another, it was a long time before he settled down to it: 'A Poet Gossips', Chapter One:

> Now shall I, before it is too late, set down in prose what I have already said in verse, to a very limited audience – God help us all ... A Scotch–Irish–Armenian brought up remorselessly and regardless of cost, as an English Gentleman, must be prepared for stormy weather, but did that really explain the number of times I found myself exhilaratingly alone, on a wind and wave swept deck, preferably with night coming on and the charts mislaid? No. But it took me some years to discover what was really wrong.

I don't think he ever did. The few pages he wrote are about Black Grandpa's life, not his own.

> And henceforward this Book will be concerned with what I have seen and heard and done and thought between the ages of four and seventy-two. . . . This book is then the testament in prose of an obscure poet set down on the very verge of his own apparent personal extinction but one who, none the less, believes in personal immortality and would like to share the glad tidings, however intrinsically terrifying, with everyone who cares to read on to the last chapter.

That was page eight. There were four more pages, still *not* about Ernest but about his father. Then a new chapter – about Aleppo:

> But meanwhile what was happening in our home? We settled outside the city walls, closely ringed by cemeteries, beyond the lush efficiently worked gardens, irrigated by the vast bulk of the city's sewage and a scanty and uncertain little river.

And that is where the book ends. All at once the stream dries up. There are only a sad little row of asterisks to mark where, suddenly, he could write no more, prevented by a blood clot on the brain.

From then on, he was a very cross invalid, lying with a rug over his knee and a dictionary under the sofa. When his brain would not produce the word he wanted, he would dive down angrily to the dictionary. Only a few weeks more of this and he died under anaesthetic while being operated on for gangrene of the leg. Roger, who was present at the operation, had to give the news to Dora. It was 1962.

It took me a long time to realize he was no longer there. After years spent reacting to his every mood, I found the sudden peace disconcerting, like when you turn a corner on a mountain walk and find yourself suddenly out of the teasing wind. He used to say that he was always tempted to disturb calm pools, throw a stone in, create ripples, so I found it hard, as I grew up, to form a very clear image of myself. And he was physically disturbing, hardly ever at peace unless absorbed. He preferred to be moving, playing tennis, riding, swimming and, most of all, dancing in his very special way. He moved across a floor with a sliding motion as if on skates, coming to rest with toes turned in and head on one side. In the hospital, he had to speak with people shorter than himself, had to bend sideways to listen to them; his one deaf ear was another result of the German shell which had permanently bent his little finger and lodged a sharp piece of metal in his body.

It was a poor funeral by Aleppo standards. No pallbearers, no line of scouts carrying wreaths, no carriages with the horses decked in black ostrich feathers, and no hearty young men carrying the coffin: just a small plain box on a rickety trolley trundled down the aisle. But Ernest would have been pleased that he had achieved one ambition, at least: to rest in Coniston, the same churchyard as the Collingwood family, in the shadow of the Old Man by the enchanted lake:

> I look across the lawn and through the four firs down to the grey lake and see the cloud ramparted by the mountains. I hear the clock tick in the silence and security that the English countryside alone can give.

But his funeral music was an Armenian lullaby.

There were touching letters from that 'hell town' now he was gone: 'Dear Dr. Roger, We mourn the death of your lovely father. What can we do in this world where sorrow and death is reigning? It is the law and order of this world.' And a former matron wrote gently, 'Poor dear, he's been through a lot and is now at rest'. A lifelong friend assured: 'Nobody will ever forget either of you, either separately or together, the absolute difference between you and the shining example of teamwork that no malice or fortune could spoil . . . Ernest that merry genius would laugh heartily at my efforts to say what I feel . . . a person like that cannot be snuffed out.' 'One of the pillars of my life', wrote another friend. Sir John Glubb, with whom Ernest had done the Iraq campaign, wrote with his usual forthrightness to *The Times*: 'I do not remember ever having met a more public spirited or more courageous man.' And he added a special letter to put the record straight:

Dr. Altounyan was neither a secret agent nor a politician. Together we acted to some extent as a connecting link between the British Army and the Syrian leaders in the Second World War and he was in the confidence of the Commander in Chief. It was his hope to see Syria independent and a friend of Britain and he never concealed this hope.

In the *Lancet*, Geoffrey Keynes, who had operated on Ernest for renal calculus, 'the common trouble of the parched lands of the Middle East', harked back to Dr. A.A. Altounyan being 'the first man to practice modern aseptic surgery in Syria . . . his extraordinary reputation created difficulties for his son who felt he could never be a worthy successor.' Of the operation, he wrote: 'He gave me precise instructions as to how the removal was to be done. I carried out his instructions to the letter.' Remembering his colleague's 'unusual and often tempestuous career', he noted that his odd blend of qualities did not seem to come to terms with themselves: 'He was highly emotional and in many ways severely practical. While he was at times deeply depressed he was resilient and could be absurdly optimistic in the face of the most adverse circumstances. In his happier moods he was a most exciting though sometimes exhausting companion.'

Exhausting sometimes, stimulating almost always. Ernest and Dora were so different, they fitted together to make a complete whole. In what was to be his last visit to Beirut, Ernest described the well-known scenery to her – the view of the bay from his hotel window – 'but I can't bear to look at it without you. It is just dust and ashes.' And Dora could not go on living alone for long, sitting by a one-bar electric heater in that morning-room where so much had happened since she had come to live there, aged about five. The family, who paid calls from time to time, scolded her for being in a draught, just as she had scolded her mother. They asked her what she was tearing up: 'Old letters'. She did not want us to have it to do when she was gone. Many letters were left, but perhaps they read a shade too blandly, perhaps she got rid of the worst ones, quarrels and unhappinesses. Perhaps that is why my father's letters to his psychologist friend, John Rickman, are raw in comparison. They were returned to me unedited, untreated.

Dora's death, in 1964, was like the fading of the last beams of the sun on the mountain. It was the end of the life the two of them had created together. Her paintings of Syria remain, incadescent embers of her excitement at first seeing olive trees behind Marseilles: 'Aleppo is more picturesque than most of the pictures of the East one sees. It is something that just catches hold of one'; 'I try to paint because I want to keep a beautiful scene. But one can't keep painting all the time and often my attempts to convey the particular feeling are a failure'. When I was last in Aleppo, someone handed me a roll of dusty sketches by Dora that he had found knocking about in the souk. Rubbish they looked, so old and tattered. But they were my mother's so I carried them back to the hotel and arranged them round the walls. And those faded watercolours and oils of the lakes my mother had packed at the bottom of her trunk sixty years before, glowed suddenly for us, shut out the heat and clamour of Aleppo. The cool fragrance of a bank of daffodils, blowing in the spring breeze, the forgotten peace of an English lake at sunset. Only a few streaks of faint colour on dusty brown paper, limp with age, but radiating energy as they faded – like a grain of radium.

PART II
Reverberations

The veil began to dissolve and part. Something struck me in my soul – like a large bell, and I just vibrated.

Alice Walker, *The Colour Purple*

Chapter Twelve

For about twenty years after my parents died I felt too angry to go back to Aleppo. But in 1979 I went back to Syria as part of an archaeological expedition. When the dig closed, I could not leave without visiting Aleppo.

The hospital was still standing but looked very tatty. It was being used as a government school. Apparently, one of the assistant doctors had removed the medical equipment, claiming that my father had given it to him. It was now all in a back-street flat with a sign over the door reading: 'The Altounyan Hospital'. Hardly trusting myself, I called on the doctor. I did not get further than the front office.

The dust lay very thickly on the huge portrait of my grandfather hanging over the desk. My mother had hated this portrait, by a Frenchman, she said, who had made his fortune in Aleppo by flattering his sitters: reducing the noses of the ladies, the waistlines of the men, giving everyone peachlike complexions. The dust lay on the doctor's desk too. He did not quite meet my eye as we sat sipping Turkish coffee, each of us waiting for the other to start speaking.

Perhaps there was a sparkling, dust-free clinic, full of fluttering nurses in crisp starched uniforms, behind those dividing doors kept so firmly closed behind the doctor. It was very likely my father had handed over the hospital and its contents to him before he left. Having had just a few days to wind up his affairs, how much time had he had to do anything else? Perhaps he had really made him his heir to spite Roger? We had heard so many rumours and counter-rumours, accusations and counter-accusations. My friends listed the betrayals and the injustices: 'all those lovely stoves your father put in, sold off'; 'the laboratory apparatus scattered'. It seemed ungrateful to our friends, who had been preserving our memory, to say I did not really care. But I was touched. Reminders would keep cutting in, sometimes painfully. In the hotel, the ancient barman had died ('They gave him the wrong blood. It would never have happened in your hospital'). The bent old lady creeping about the marble halls upstairs greeted me like a long lost sister: 'I remember you on your wedding day. Oh why are your cheeks now so withered?' Where, for that matter, was the sprightly, black-eyed chambermaid who had brought us our first married breakfast? And all the time I avoided the street where our house had been taken stone from stone, as efficiently as when Hülegü, Genghis Khan's grandson, destroyed the city in the thirteenth century. I ignored the school, with its shabby banners and crumbling air, which had been our hospital, but I visited my grandfather's grave, lying so modestly in the shadow of the church. Everything seemed very black. At first I thought it was because the trees had grown up but then I saw that the stones themselves were black with fungus, as if they had been standing in water too long and rotted. The whole town was afflicted with this car pollution, although only at street level, fortunately. The castle, aloof on its hill, still floated like a golden crown, the famous Aleppo stone still responding to the times of day, through dawn grey to the white heat of noon to the flush of sunset. And in spite of the efforts of developers, the town as a whole still had its dignity, its 'beauté mâle et grave', as Sauvaget has it. A 'handmade' town that has taken so long to put together takes a long time to fall apart. Pockets of ancient history remain. An ambitious town mayor who, needless to say, was not Aleppo-born – he came from Der Ez Zor – sought immortality for himself by taking out Bab el Faraj, the town's Piccadilly Circus. All those little shops, more shacks than shops, huddling round the edges of that open space, with the clock tower in the middle, have been bulldozed away. The pungent nut-sellers, the warm bakeries, the ecstatic cook-shops and the clinically clean baklava shops, preserving their marble coolness in the middle of all the dirt and bustle, the preserved-fruit boxes heaped round the entrances, holes in the walls which called themselves shops, have all gone and in their stead stands a huge monument (insulting to the glorious stone of Aleppo) inscribed with the name of the mayor and the legend, 'It is the will of the people'. Next to Barons Hotel an old house is being rooted out like a rotten tooth. The machines work at night, by floodlight, as if in a hurry, but work stops when something is found, a Roman glass bottle perhaps, – it might be valuable!

The New Aleppo is now being built on the rocky hills to the north-west of the town. In the old days the American College for Boys shared this wilderness only with bedouin tents, dogs and rubbish heaps. My mother and I wandered there sometimes in search of red anemonies. A few yards of carefully made road was called the 'tour de ville' in the hope that, some day, it might even reach the back of the citadel where no 'civilized' person dared go. The new stone villas had lawns and herbacious borders. Water has worked the miracle. Since the great Assad reservoir has been built, Aleppo can show off with water, build the great dual carriageway bordered with grass and flowers that every Syrian town now has.

In the new houses on the hill live young men passionate about Aleppo, her past and her future. Some of them are French, some American, some Arab, all with work in the city, *not* tourists. Pierre, a planner married to a girl from Homs who he had met at a French university where she was studying linguistics, was my host for several evenings. His wife, balancing herself on a carved capital filched from some Byzantine ruin near Aleppo, was beautifully pregnant. With her straight Greek nose and hanging ear-rings, she reminded me of a figure on a Palmyrine tomb. As I struggled through that traditional Aleppo soup, which seems to be made of stinging nettles and egg white, the young men and I exchanged information about the past and the present. After supper we sat on the floor over a heap of old photographs: 'Where is this?' 'Who is this?' I realized, yet again, what a sheltered, unadventurous life I had lead in the old days. I knew nothing then of what was on the other side of the castle. It might as well have been the other side of the moon. We went out every afternoon, but in the car, usually accompanied by a nurse and a driver. We left the car at the entrance to the old city but, now and then, we thought it fun to urge the driver through the narrowest streets. No wonder the little boys threw stones, and the grown-ups cursed as they flattened themselves out of our way. The old doctor, twenty years before, visiting patients on his horse, was one thing, but this car with all the windows tightly closed, full of jeering children, was quite another.

But Pierre and his friends were not shocked. I was 'an artifact'. It amused them to show me the public baths I had never been in. Did I know why they were now so far below the street? Because they were much older than the present street. They showed me the entrances to underground passages which, they said, formed a secret network under the town. They took me to dark caves in which gigantic vats were cooking beans, the traditional food of the Aleppo poor. They took me into the tanning factory which I had known only as 'the worst smell in town' – any one of us who could pass it without holding their nose got a prize! I saw unpicturesque warrens full of pale children making lovely carpets. We went into ancient houses, perhaps not as grand, but just as lovely in their humbler way, as the famous ones I already knew. And when we wandered round Azizieh, where we used to live together, I saw the familiar homes of our old friends from the outside, appreciated their architecture, no longer wrapped in a shy dread of afternoon calls and having to speak so many languages. They told me that the wooden fronts to these old houses are now irrestorable and I was glad. I had always felt menaced by eyes behind shutters, the veiled faces of Muslim patients who sat waiting for the doctors in our hall. There was very little privacy in our young lives; perhaps we did not miss it but, at times, the roof seemed to be the only place where one was not observed. Our enormous rooms did have doors, but they were hardly ever shut.

It was the short season of fresh pistachio nuts which, in Aleppo, is almost a festival. As we sat and talked, the tables round us and the marble floors were awash with sunset-coloured skins. Our hands and breath took on a tang which was more subtle than the smell of pine.

As the road away from Aleppo became an endless repetition of telegraph poles past the car windows I felt free. Damascus, smelling of white jasmine, meant anonymity, not having to play the old role still imperative in my home town. The ghosts were left behind.

Many childhood playmates, old friends had gone to Soviet Armenia in 1946. We had heard nothing from them. It was as if they had gone into the mountain after the Pied Piper. But in 1969 I had published a book, called *In Aleppo Once*, and had some money of my own. By coincidence, it was just enough to pay for a journey to Soviet Armenia. By another coincidence, that year the country felt ready to receive visitors.

The world was informed that Soviet Armenia was now celebrating 2,750 years of the history of the Urartian town of Erebuni, the old name for Yerevan, the present capital of Soviet Armenia. No one, except archaeologists, had then heard of Urartu, but now we learned that the Urartians, who had established themselves round Van (their capital) in the second millennium, used an adapted form of cuneiform for their inscriptions. In the past they had been confused with their enemies, the Assyrians. The Armenians, who had the same skills of stonemasonry and metalwork, were not the same people and only became important a thousand years later.

Urartian history is best grasped obliquely, like trying to count the stars in the Seven Sisters constellation. The excavations at Erebuni had revealed a magnificent palace with rich golden treasure. It was an occasion for rejoicing and showing off the new Armenian state. The magic date '2750' in great Soviet cut-out quite dwarfed the little airport buildings.

There were seven of us on that 1969 autumn tour to Moscow and Yerevan (travelling fearfully and not very hopefully). There were two elderly ladies, their iron-grey hair covered in black shawls or *vellos*, like my Aleppo nurses used to wear when they went out, their lined faces set in a resolve to bear anything. A married couple looked almost as miserable, though the wife wore a hat covering a fashionable perm, and a fur collar to her expensive coat. She had the air of a Pekinese about to be sick. Her little husband kept his hat on, even at mealtimes, its wide brim well pulled down over his long nose. He never spoke a word in public – in any language. I expected more from an elderly bachelor; his hair cut short like an American, gave him quite a worldly air, but his initial spriteliness soon became an annoying fussiness, a paranoic suspicion of everybody and everything. The life and soul was a flirtatious lady in her forties, travelling without her husband and making the most of it. But even she became devious when we got to currency declarations. I was the only one not entirely Armenian. This seemed to make me guide and unofficial translator. Although all of us had well-worn British passports, suddenly no one else had a word of English. The young Russian at my elbow insisted on me writing 'none' in full opposite 'anything to declare?' on all the forms. Sometimes I wrote in '*voch*' in Armenian just to vary it a bit! 'Why does no one speak Armenian?' muttered the old ladies, drawing their black shawls across their mouths. 'When shall we be free of this terrible country?' There were several thousand square miles of that terrible country, stretching all round us, Armenia being just a small section at least a thousand miles to the south of Moscow. Would we survive the journey? In London I had found it difficult enough to think of Armenia as a real country, on a map, with an airport, a mean summer and winter temperature . . . But here was the tiny plane which was going to take us there. We followed Tania, our guide, timidly through the Russian airport officials standing like granite statues in their maxi-coats. The wind was icy. 'Perhaps the Russians don't feel the cold', we murmured. 'Cold is cold everywhere, I think', said Tania. Thin ice in puddles crackled under our feet. Inside, the plane was shabby and smelt of bodies, which did not inspire confidence. Creaking baskets and odorous bundles were wedged in everywhere, but at least the air hostess spoke proper Armenian, though with an 'Eastern' accent. We had never heard any sort of Armenian spoken over a Tannoy before. We had three hours of flying over country flat as a carpet with, here and there, sketched-in rivers and patches of silver birch in snow-shaving-cream on a stubbly chin. Then the carpet wrinkled into the Caucasus, peaked into Mount Ararat. Rain-sodden mist whipped past the window, the little plane lurched about like a lift cut loose, a last heave over the Caucasus and Yerevan was beneath us like a jewelled brooch in the darkness.

Warm air smelling of roses soothed us as we walked from the

plane through lush summer gardens full of people in thin clothes. But we only had eyes for the neon signs – in Armenian. As the saying went, 'And policemen, officials, everyone, talk Armenian'. There was only one hotel in Yerevan in 1969: the Armenia, taking up one whole side of the main square. As we whirled through the great revolving doors, we were lost in the waiting crowd. The little man with the hat was seized and danced away by a long-lost brother. His hat came off – at last – as they did a waltz round the foyer, hugging and kissing each other, laughing and crying at the same time, making up for nearly a lifetime of separation. Others were led away, giggling weakly, by pretty mothers carrying babies, and eager young men anxious for their children to do them credit in front of visiting grandparents. In the morning, I drew aside my curtains and found snowy Ararat glistening in the sun, surely just outside. Every cigarette packet in Yerevan has 'Massis' (the Armenian name for Ararat) on both sides but, unfortunately, the mountain is now in Turkey.

No sign of all those children gone into the mountain nearly twenty years ago. Marie? Zaven? Haigaz? And little Yervant? Perhaps none of them had survived.

It was easy enough to find Tatoul, Black Grandpa's nephew by the brother who had been 'cut down'. He had escaped north into the part of Russia which became Soviet Armenia. He was director of the state folk dance and opera company. I only had to ring him (telephone and electricity free as air and efficient) and he was knocking on my door five minutes later. In his hand a bath plug – I had complained that mine had disappeared. It was so familiar, the way he carefully fitted the plug before he embraced me and began to ask a thousand questions. He looked like his uncle though clean shaven, and I found it hard to understand his Armenian, partly because I was so enchanted listening to the melody, the unfamiliar words and intonation. The wool sweater I had chosen so carefully in London was tossed aside, still in its brown paper. I had been warned not to giftwrap; any windfall always had to be hidden away from jealous eyes. On the way to the opera house he was greeted at every step, just as my grandfather would have been had he ever gone on foot through Aleppo. 'Tatoul Jan' they called him or

'Tatoul Ingerr', any excuse to talk to the famous man, no matter if a desperate hen hanging upside down fluttered and flapped or a little boy wriggled impatiently. We passed a sweetshop and my arms, like a little girl's, were full of packets of sweets. 'This is my niece from Aleppo', he kept saying, and the dancing girls and the young musicians in the opera smiled indulgently and looked curious for, after all, they did not see people from *ardahsahman* (abroad) very often. In his flat, spacious and comfortable, the dresser displayed rows of bottles, whisky, gin, sherry – 'you see, I collect them' – none of them open as far as I could see. We only drank a sweet wine diluted with soda water. There was a case of conductor's batons in gold, ivory and other precious stuff, that had been presented to him all over the world. But he did not think he would be let out again. He was fond enough, he said, of his holiday cruises to the Black Sea. His wife was Russian, he had two handsome violinist sons, and a daughter who was a scientist. I managed to understand when she told me of how she had started out as a ballet dancer but one day an unconquerable fit of stage fright had made her run off in the middle of a performance, never to return. We were pleased to feel ourselves so closely related. But, when I mentioned the new immigrants from Syria, the temperature dropped. They were troublemakers. 'Don't let them come near me', Tatoul said grimly. Through all the friendliness I sensed a sudden resentment: had Assadour, his uncle, never replied to appeals for help in those terrible early days when grass soup was all the surviving refugees had to eat and no houses to protect them from the Russian winter? I knew that my grandfather, too, could be hard on occasion, disconcertingly unsentimental, no beating about the bush. But the coldness didn't last long. He was soon all right, his huge television permanently on – the Russians had just gone into space.

The Armenians who had arrived in 1946 were still longing for the country they had just left and comparing their new home unfavourably with it all the time. Although they were free to travel over most of Russia, they longed for *ardahsahman*. The younger generation was beginning to get impatient with the dreary nostalgia of its elders.

Reverberations

It was nearly dark when I at last found Zaven in his village a few miles outside Yerevan. He had been a childhood friend who worked in the hospital and lived in our house. In a car which seemed to have square wheels, we had rattled along a dirt road and stopped in front of what looked at first like a used-car dump. An apparent corpse lay underneath one of the cars. When shouted at, it picked itself up. The face was black, covered in oil. And the eyes – would they ever stop staring? We should have warned him! We made our way under a vine into the house to a large drawing-room with bright red shiny linoleum on the floor and, as usual, beds. In the days before the sofabed, every room in Yerevan was always taken up with beds, sometimes even the kitchen. After a while Zaven, washed, came in, shook hands and sat down as near to me as he could. His face had not really changed so much in twenty years. He had a moustache now, but still the same Charlie Chaplin black-rimmed dark-blue eyes, the cheeky turned-up nose unusual in an Armenian. And he had needed that cheek. Seven years in the salt mines of northern Siberia had been his lot. 'The sun in summer went round and round over my head and never set', he told me. The train journey there had taken, as far as he could calculate, three months. Luckily he was unmarried at the time. I recognized his wife as another of our hospital nurses. 'Zaven has never stopped talking about you all', she said. The two little boys clung to their mother like limpets, refusing to look up and show their faces. But gradually Zaven got used to me. With his ancient car he came and fetched me each morning from the Hotel Armenia. Together we visited churches in out-of-the-way valleys which I would never have seen but for him. Dating from the sixth century sometimes, they were unrestored, even the tiles intact on the conicle roofs. At man-height were often small crosses like kisses carved, congealed candle grease, burnt feathers on ancient thresholds. Through the padlocked gates all we could see was pigeon droppings and rubble. These churches, some pepperpot small, some great cathedrals, rear up against the stark mountainous landscape all over Armenia, on passes, by lakes, often away from human habitation. They are awe-inspiring witnesses of the time when, a thousand years ago,

Armenia was the first country in the world to adopt Christianity as its state religion. Hundreds of years later they influenced the style we know as Romanesque, away to the West in Europe. I found that, in my excitement, I had taken at least a dozen pictures of the same little church.

Up a long valley over bone-shaking roads we visited the memorial to Antranik, Armenia's most beloved guerrilla leader. His name still reverberates in the history of eastern Turkey: Zangezoor Erzurum – resounding through the highlands for ever more. Born in Shabin Karahisar, he began his activities in Sivas in 1888 (the year before my father was born). Wherever there was action, there was Antranik: he was leader of the guerrilla forces in Samsun, with thirty-eight villages under his command; besieged in a monastery (near Moush) by the Turks, he broke out, he and his men wearing the uniforms of Turkish officers; he fought countless engagements against the Turks and helped in the Macedonian struggle with a troop of Armenian volunteers in the first Balkan war. On the north Persian front he helped the Russians at Shahpur; he was Commander of the Western Armenian Division during the short-lived Dashnak republic of 1918–20, angry with his leaders for handing over oil-rich Batum to the Turks. He was about to march on Karabagh, the area which is now being disputed, when a message from the British Commander asked him to desist with a promise that the matter would be settled later. He and my grandfather were at the 1919 Versailles conference, he doing his best to persuade the allies to occupy Turkey. When he died in Fresno, California, that heaven to so many Armenian emigrants, an attempt was made to bury him in Soviet Armenia but he only got as far as Père Lachaise cemetery in Paris. Zaven and I found his bust surrounded by wreaths and secret signs of independence in that remote valley.

I met so many other old friends in Yerevan. I found it hard to have to eat more than two meals a day (and such lavish meals, all that anyone remembered I had been fond of). By the time I left, my throat was scraped sore with harsh unaccustomed Armenian. I went on talking about Armenia when I got back for much too long for all my English friends. Zaven wrote me long letters in English, though we had talked

Armenian together. He had only heard us speaking English to each other, more than twenty years ago, never pronounced the words, just as I had Turkish stored up in my head. And at Christmas there arrived a parcel from Yerevan, quite unlike any of the other parcels we got that year, or any other year. A small wooden box, tied with string, with the ink of the address running in long lines along the grain of the wood so that it was hardly legible, and in the wrong order – 'England' first, ending with the surname. Somewhere, between Yerevan and London, the tiny packing case had started to come apart, and had been repaired with more string and much too large nails. One cut with scissors and it all fell apart, a lot of brown tissue paper rustled out, released from the buffeting of its 2,000-mile journey. It was strangely dung-coloured and drab, no bright papers, or ribbons, or silly cards – they would have been thought too frivolous in the Soviet Union. On my bare polished table: one small plastic bag full of raisins; a square of dried apricots; a stick of *sujuk*, nuts that have been threaded on a string and dipped again and again in a mixture of grape juice and starch, then hung up to dry. Before they had fridges the villagers had to work all the year round preparing food for the winter that would not go bad. Also in the parcel were some broken pieces of plaster, too crumbly to put together, but representing the Holy Church of Etchmiazin. A letter on thin grey writing paper carried Armenian Christmas greetings. I remembered how, under our Christmas tree in Aleppo, I had, one Christmas, found a wooden comb from the souk, some gritty native soap and a coarse napkin, hand woven, presents from an old missionary lady. I'm still surprised how shocked I was.

Zaven had told me in 1969 that he had a van ready fitted-up to make the journey from Russia to England if he ever got a permit. But he was not able to get out until 1988, when he went to America. Perhaps he expected us to be as we had been all those years ago. He knew I was divorced and living alone, but my whole flat would have fitted into one room of our house in Aleppo and I did not even have a 'cleaning lady'. When we sent him a group photograph of Roger's sixty-fifth birthday party (taken the year before he died) he complained that we all looked so old. We found it hard to recognize the picture he sent us of himself at his son's wedding.

While I was growing up in Aleppo, Turkey, the enemy country, was for me as remote as a continent separated by oceans. We were physically barred from travelling there and psychologically prevented from asking questions. So I had no sense of time or space. The frontier was ten or a hundred miles away; the tragedy could have happened ten or a hundred years ago. It was like being in Bluebeard's palace with that locked room inviting and repelling.

At the age of thirteen, just as I might have started to ask real questions and demand answers, I was sent off to school in England, where I foundered in a sea of new problems and had no time to think about Armenians. There remained a vague mixture of fascination and unease – and guilt. And then we siblings were scattered and did not have much opportunity to talk to each other.

Two things happened: in his late fifties Roger was very depressed for a few months. As he recovered we were more able to talk to each other. He told me that he had always had a nightmare: Turks handing him a glass of Armenian blood to sip. He made a comic face expecting me to laugh. But I remembered how, as a small boy at Lanehead (after we had all been sent to boarding school), he had always been strangely frightened about going upstairs to bed alone – because of wolves, he said. So he too had been carrying about in the back of his mind the memory of stories told to him which he had been forbidden to pass on.

The second thing was I had vaguely thought that the massacres had happened too long ago for there to be any survivors. Then I met an Armenian family in London who became real friends. The mother, only a little older than me, told me she had been in Aleppo as a small girl of about five at the time I had first arrived there with my parents. She and her family were being deported and like crowds of others were on their way to the desert through Aleppo. By a stroke of good luck they had been saved. She told me about visiting her mother in my grandfather's hospital and of her great surprise in finding her on an iron bedstead. Even well-off families, in those days, spread their bedding on the floor at night rolling it up and putting it away in a wall cupboard. So meeting a survivor of my own age I realized that there must be many more. I could now ask questions. I began to feel more at ease with the part of me that was 'Hai'.

So Sivas existed and I had to go there.

Thanks to marrying an Englishman, my name was no longer Armenian. But where had I learned all that Turkish? Evening classes, because Anatolia was so interesting archaeologically. Old ladies are almost invisible in Turkey and, if noticed, are treated kindly. A package tour seemed at first a peculiar way of getting back. Black Grandpa would not have understood. But I did not dare risk delays in Turkish police posts, possible nights in Turkish prisons. I determined to keep my mouth shut, not easy when my room-mate was already declaring that she was 'in love with the Turks'. I remembered my mother's set face if anyone said such a thing at our dinner table. She did not usually let herself express violent emotions, she left that to my father. But the Turks ... 'Beujuks', she would say with a peculiar vehemence, meaning simply 'bedbug'. And I remember the tone of her voice, when she said 'Der Ez Zor', jolted my infant feelings, but I did not know why. I did not know that Der Ez Zor on the Euphrates was then an extermination camp where thousands of Armenians driven down from eastern Turkey drowned in the river, if they had survived the deportation. The river must have seemed a restful end to those poor women and children. Aleppo was a staging post; many died in its streets. Black Grandpa's nephew, a few years older than me, now remembers how his bicycle bumped casually over dead bodies on his way to school, and lorries drove through the streets piled with bodies.

The joyful year Ernest and Dora were married in Coniston was the start of the agony. When we arrived in Aleppo, the eyes of those around us were still wide with horror, their minds still shaking, preoccupied, maimed. Perouz was my first nurse – a great mountain woman from Kharpert. We sometimes slept in the same room and she shouted at me when I coughed. Faded snaps show her at Coniston sailing with us, holding our hands as we ventured into the cold cold lake. Our worst fear was being thrown in by Ernest. My mother must have chosen Perouz because the best Armenian was spoken where she came from, it had been a university town. In Kharpert, before the massacres, 13,000 stalwart Armenians carried guns for the Turks against the Russians. Disarmed, they were led away in batches and shot. There was a more sophisticated death for the intellectuals: they were hung by the arms for a day and night, fingernails and hair pulled out, watching their friends beaten to death. Last, the women and children were turned out into the desert and directed south, preyed upon all the way. Shame forced them to walk bent double because they were by then naked, their clothes stolen. Stumbling on through bitter cold and scorching sun, thirst was their last torture. Any hope of drinking turned them wild: women threw themselves recklessly into any wells, drowned in any water, faces pressed into the mud by those behind. If any should manage to crawl out, dripping, they were mobbed by crazed licking tongues. Bodies rotted in the water and no one cared.

Another nurse, Makrouhi, came from Maras, which was nearer Aleppo, a hundred miles to the north. The very year we arrived, the town had been caught in the last fighting between French and Turkish troops. The Armenians trusted the French but they withdrew, suddenly, secretly, by night. A few thousand managed to struggle after the retreating army, leaving Maras behind them in flames. In front were only arid gorges, winter blizzards raging. Most of those who did manage to get within sight of Aleppo were hacked to pieces. Makrouhi told us of babies taken from their mothers' arms, heads smashed against rocks, pregnant women with their stomachs split. 'But *hsss* don't tell your mother.' after a moment we went back to splashing in our baths, teasing Makrouhi, who giggled so deliciously. It had only happened to dolls, not us.

The package tour, in 1983, took me to Urfa. All we children had been allowed to know was that Urfa women were fond of pale blue and wore a peculiar azure *sharval*. We met them walking into Aleppo in cheerful groups from New Urfa, clean and windy on the hill. But I could not eat when we lunched in ancient Urfa, under the trees by the pond, in the shadow of the citadel. I could follow Turkish women into the darkness of the souk, buy their fine wool togas which enveloped them so majestically from the summit of their high pointed head-dresses to their coy slippers. On the creamy wool were scattered joyful flowers, sky blue. But, in the pool, the swarming carp, writhing as they caught our crumbs, were people drowning.

There were frequent and cheap buses from Ankara to Sivas. I was put in the best seat as all old ladies are in Turkey. Next to me was a pleasant woman in the usual shawl which, from old habit, she kept half covering her face. Women are not supposed to be veiled these days. I pretended I knew no Turkish as the journey was to take six hours. We sat most of the way with her little grandson's sleeping head on my lap. But she was not going to let language be a barrier. Now and then she dived into the bag at her feet and fished out something to eat – I was always given some. She kept smoothing my arm, testing the material of my clothes, examining my hands, and then she had to find out if I was married. She swept the fingers of one hand under her nose, suggesting a curling moustache. But I did not understand her.

There had been many more villages in my grandfather's day, more animation to the scene, more farm traffic on the roads, but the outline of the low hills where he must have wandered with his catapult was the same, as was the river. A modern road led straight to the modern town centre where my hotel was; I might have been anywhere in Anatolia. I made for the central square, the Seljuk mosque. Assadour must have knocked his ball up against its walls when no one was looking, perhaps squatted, sheltered in the entrance, and played knucklebones with his pals on the way back from school. There was no sign of any Armenian church but there was a rockery where I knew one of them had stood. In a back street I picked an old prosperous-looking house for the Altounyans' and sat down on a stone outside the closed gate. There was no one in the little square but soon I heard the sound of a flute and a boy came round the corner with a small flock of sheep. He took them inside the compound so I had a chance to look: a garden, stables for the animals, the family living upstairs, a balcony with a wooden rail running round the house, and a red-tiled roof. In the emptiness and peace it was easy to imagine the scene at the gate as the doctor's caravan set out for Aintab: the loaded carts, the mules and donkeys, and the horses for the 'gentry' to ride. My great-grandmother weeping – it was the last time she was to see her son.

The Armenians had put up some sort of resistance at Sivas when the trouble began. It was said that Armenian bakers had been poisoning the bread supplied to the Turkish army. The leaders of this resistance had managed to get away to the Black Sea and then by boat to Europe, but mass deportation was the fate of most of the Armenians in the town and surrounding villages. Of the 160,000 deported, only 10,000 survived – and, evidently, old women had no hope.

It was the festival of Bairam in Sivas when I was there, and the walls and street corners were drenched in sheep's blood. Every family has to kill. Lorries toured the streets, the fat butcher standing in the back sharpening his knives shouting for custom. After the killing was done, the absorbed crowd would disperse and the butcher would throw the bloody fleece into the back of the truck and drive on.

Because it was Bairam, the whole town was shopping and anyone who had anything to sell displayed it – on the ground, on barrows, on the outside walls, on flat roofs, anywhere. Postcards by the yard formed a sort of tapestry wherever there was space, and there were trays full of rubbishy rings – I spent a long time choosing one which disintegrated the next day. But I bought a quince off a barrow which scented my luggage all the way back to London. Lots of strange wild fruits, nuts, bulbs and grasses were being sold in twists of newspaper by children. I bought the fruit of the wild strawberry tree or arbutus. It tasted bland like a tinned lychee. The richer shops, which were hardly more than holes, overflowed into the road so that it was hard to walk: there were mountains of watermelons, heaps of cabbages, sacks full of anything that could be gathered and sold. There were little girls selling water from the kerbside, old men sitting hopefully beside weighing machines or touting single grubby bus tickets at bus stops. I never did find out how they made money that way. Shoeshine boys were everywhere, of course, and boys guarding what cars there were while their owners sat in restaurants. Trays of cold tea swung through the crowds, carried by yet more ambitious small boys. Always the sign of a poor country, children trying to pick up a kurus here and there and looking so miserably starved.

Beautiful old *kilims*, some of them tattered, were always being unfolded at my feet by men as old as I was, who hoped I was German. They had spent a lot of their youth working in Germany and were longing to talk. But I wanted socks, handknitted woollen socks. I did not hope to find any with crosses on the toes like in the old days but, Christian or Moslem, no one ever dreams of stepping inside a house with shoes on. So socks are still important. Instead of crosses you find every sort of design from centuries back, even the Greek gioche pattern. Socks were to be bought everywhere and usually appeared when it was plain I would not buy carpets. I found some in a cave selling nothing but rock salt. When the sack was emptied out contemptuously into the dust, most of them were odd sizes and some of the feet were ridiculously small. Had Ghenghis Khan brought the custom of foot binding with him from China?

There were some beautiful socks, some of them even with crosses on the toes, in a glass case in one of the rooms of the Seljuk mosque which had been turned into a museum. A very old man was sitting in a sunny corner with a young man standing respectfully by. I saw that he was translating something from the old Arabic script into modern Turkish. Only the very old know how to do that these days. Atatürk brought in the Latin script to show that Turkey was now really part of Europe. Also sitting in the autumn sunlight with nothing to do to justify their badges ('Official Guide'), were friendly girls. I suddenly found I knew quite a lot of Turkish. Here I could really be an archaeologist. They had broad mountain-peasant faces and boasted to me happily about the cold winters, just as my grandfather used to do. This seems to be the dividing line between desert Arab, to whom snow only comes rarely as a calamity, and the Turks and Armenians and other peoples of the hills, to whom it is a yearly fact of life. I could hardly believe my nurse's stories – told in waterless Aleppo – about gushing rivers and pine woods. Strange that, in the unforgettable year my grandfather died, his native weather came south – icefloes in the Euphrates (they may have started in central Anatolia where the river rises) and such deep snow in the Syrian desert that only the tops of the telegraph poles showed where the road was. Perhaps love of snow and mountains formed the real bond of understanding between Black Grandpa and White Grandpa.

All the time I was in Sivas I was careful not to mention that I was in the smallest bit Armenian. But on my last day I met a small boy in the park who told me in perfect English that he and his family had just come back from working in Australia. Because he spoke English and not Turkish, he told me he was taken for an ... Armenian! Meaning someone strange and foreign. I shared with him the bag of sweets I had been handed as I left the hotel that morning. Everyone was being given sweets in Sivas that day – even Armenians.

Erzurum was the next stop on our package tour. It had always been the key to Anatolia, overrun by every hoard from the east, every army, suffering massacre after massacre, breeding the most beautiful women, the bravest men. Erzurum women still walked with a special pride even in the streets of Aleppo, even in their ragged refugee clothes, and sang about their home in a way to break your heart.

Winter was eight months long in Erzurum, longer than most invaders could endure. The streets were glaciers, the town an ice fortress. They say a cat could be caught by the cold on a roof, remain frozen all the winter, and come to life again in the spring.

The mountains were already striped white, like great snow tigers, when we circled and landed that October. Baby soldiers, fresh faced and friendly, cradling their guns lovingly, grinned at our ridiculous clothes – didn't we know that Erzurum was *saook* – cold? We bought up every woollen shawl in the souk and wrapped ourselves, shivering. Some of the women wore the Urfa toga but here it was dark brown and might have been chiffon in the icy wind. We had only one day here to see everything in between crowding desperately into tea places to recuperate. Through the dusk and chill we saw Seljuk mosques as elaborately carved as Far Eastern temples, and Seljuk tombs which copied the Armenian church drum and pointed roof, at least a half millennium older. Our modern hotel was outside the old town on the edge of the wilderness which once had been alive with Armenian villages. Now it was only a scalding emptiness.

The next day we came to the end of the important-looking tarmac road a few miles out of Erzurum and, for the rest of our journey to the frontier, were enveloped in thick clouds of dust, our heads wrapped in our shawls. We met only lorries and wooden ox carts with solid spokeless wheels like the ancient carts fished up recently out of Armenian lakes, thousands of years old. The costumes of families who filled the carts, like bright bedding plants, could not have changed very much – gathered skirts and full trousers, short jackets, seams as simple as possible, different lengths of material covering sometimes only the head, sometimes the whole body – the simple alphabet of costume with regional variations, small but vitally important, all over the world where climate makes dress necessary.

As we drove towards the Russian frontier, our guide became more and more jumpy. Please don't even point your camera towards Russia – 'Where is Russia?' 'Over there . . . don't look that way.' We were all eager to see Ararat and became excited at every snowy peak. 'You'll know when you see it', said Ingrid with the smile of one who has glimpsed heaven. And when it came time for lunch there was Ararat looming over us, just across two fields – or so it looked. Ingrid had to hold us ramblers back from starting for the top: 'It is much further than it looks'. The little stream we washed our plates in was the mighty River Araxes, or Aras, 'Mother of Armenia'. When I picked up a large lump of lava that looked like a petrified pink sponge, I could believe that it had erupted from the bowels of Ararat. The mountainsides were streaked with lava only just cooled. We had passed fields of petrified glass obsidian – lying about disregarded now, but as rare and valuable as gold in the days before steel. Like maddened gold-diggers, we had filled our pockets with the stuff and then jettisoned most of it on our way back to the bus. My treasured piece of pearly grey glass was handflaked how many thousand years ago? Hittites, Mitanians,

Hurrians: ancient names, but we knew them; many more tribes had wandered across those plains and were now completely forgotten. The word for 'apple' is the same in Armenian and Hurrian, but who worries about their fate today? Why could not the Armenians vanish as they did?

Each hour in the dusty bus took us nearer the north-eastern frontier. We stopped the night at Kars, only carts and horses and occasional buses, like ours, discharging their passengers on to carts which took them to isolated villages. Rows of little shops clustered around the 'modern' 1930s hotel; at dusk the sound of shutters being pulled down; flocks of geese being driven through the muddy streets, puddles sometimes deep enough for them to swim in. Finding our way to the restaurant in the dark, we tried to walk on pavements which were nothing but perilous kerbstones. Perhaps the paving had been stolen. We climbed up a ramp to the brooding castle, past long low peasants' houses, prettily washed in blue and pink, clinging to the side of the cliff like swallows' nests. The name of Colonel Williams was still remembered in connection with the castle. As usual, the Armenians had been left between the cracks while Turks, Russians, French and British fought it out. They were often in a quandary when the European powers supported Turkey against Russia; the Armenians in Turkey could find themselves fighting against their countrymen in Russia. Kars, with its neat Russian suburb and tumbledown Turkish town, expresses this ambivalence. It changed hands several times: it was Ottoman until 1879; Russian from 1879 to 1918; Armenian from 1918 to 1920; and since 1920 it has been Turkish.

But we were only in Kars because we wanted to go to Ani. Our passports were taken away because Ani is on the frontier with Russia. I was relieved to have mine back as I had done a tiny hatchet job, changing my Armenian name 'Taqui' to 'Jaqui'.

The City of a Thousand Churches is today a desert no man's land, with a deep ravine running through it, dividing Russia from Turkey. Barbed-wire frontier posts gaze at each other across the gap and between them, on the edge of giddy precipices, totter the remains of thousand-year-old cathedrals and churches. The deep cracks that sometimes split them from roof to floor might well have been caused by the last earthquake, but no one cares and no one has the power to do anything. Photography is usually forbidden, so the outside world gets very little idea of what is happening. Escorted by Turkish soldiers in front and behind, we were hardly allowed to pause and never to pick anything up. They prudently stayed outside if we wandered into a church, risking our heads under a tottering wall, gazing down an abyss trying to identify broken carvings which had either been thrown or fallen there. I thought of Durham Cathedral, far away at the other end of Christendom, which had been built at about the same time. That cherished building with its tea shop, its gift shop . . .

Ani represents a brief high point in Armenian history when the King Ashod of the Baghratuni family was able, in 922, to take on the title of King of Kings over the other Caucasian kings. For a century after that, according to ancient Armenian scribes, 'Princes with joyous countenances sat on the princely thrones, they were clad in brilliant colours and looked like spring gardens. The sound of flutes, of cymbals and of other instruments filled one's heart with the comfort of great joy.' But it was too good to last: first the Seljuk Turks and then the Mongols attacked not a hundred years later. The walls still look solid enough but not many of the thousand churches remain. A rich orange glow lit the whole sad scene as we left, me walking backwards as I knew I would never come there again.

On the way to Van, we drove through Bitlis, a claustrophobic town hanging on the side of a deep gorge. Sitting in the bus, we had to strain our necks to see the sky. When Ingrid looked nervous and warned us not to wander about, I remembered that it was here that Grandpa's uncle had been killed – 'cut down in front of his family' – two years before I was born. I know now that 'butcher battalions' had systematically shot all the men, distributed the better-looking women and children among the soldiers, and driven the 'useless ones' on into the desert towards Aleppo and the Euphrates.

The town of Van had a slightly different history. As far back as 1869, the fiery patriarch, Khrimian, had 'awakened the community to a sense of nationhood'. It helped that, in the town, Armenians were in the majority over the Turks. When, in

1915, the usual murdering began, under pretext of searching for arms, the Armenians were cool enough to set about organizing their defence. Walls were built, and inside walls, secret passages were tunnelled under Turkish strongholds, one of which was in the American Consulate. But the Turks were in possession of the great rock cliff towering above the huddled town (in Urartian times a rock-cut passage had been the only entrance to the capital), so they were able to throw down bombs and the defenders were hampered by panicking refugees flooding in from the surrounding countryside. They clogged up the warrenlike streets, ate the remaining food – snow and flower-bulbs were all there was left. But after five weeks' siege, the Turks unexpectedly began to evacuate their women and children across the lake in boats, load their canons on to the back of mules and leave. The Russians arrived quickly – a brief respite; time for the keys of the town to be triumphantly handed over by the Armenians. But, barely six weeks later, famine and extreme cold defeated even the Russians, who were again retreating – as usual trailing with them thousands of scared refugees. The Turks moved in again and slaughtered any that remained.

The great cliff of Van rises several hundred feet over what used to be the dense Armenian town. Today, there is nothing but a pockmarked graveyard, a rubbish heap. The only standing building is a mosque. The ancient kings of Urartu were entombed in chambers and galleries hollowed out in the sheer cliff face and this was where the last battles were fought out, the wounded hurled to their death down the cliff. Human sacrifices were performed in the temple on the summit in prehistoric times. Channels were carved in the rocks for the blood to run down and they are still there.

But it all looked very calm and quiet the day we were there. The soda-blue waters of the lake reflected snow-topped mountains rising from the opposite shore and near the gemlike island with its little pepperpot church which every Armenian has in his mind's eye, although very few can now visit it. The little boat which was to take us across was belching a cloud of black smoke. As I dressed on the beach after a swim in the soapy soda-milk water, I saw at my feet not a shell or a pebble but a bone, dazzling white against the volcano-black beach. I picked it up lightheartedly, thinking it must belong to some animal. But it might well be human. As I climbed down into the boat, the Kurdish boatman shouted to his assistant on the shore: 'look at this old bag. What is she doing travelling from home at her age?' Suddenly there seemed to be a shadow over the sun. Perhaps my Armenian friend was right, I should not have come to this horrible place. The boat did look perilously low in the water. Perhaps they plotted to drown us – or to drown just me; I was the only Armenian. Surely they had not found out my secret? I thought of all the bones that must lie at the bottom of the lake. And now I heard the same man boasting of how he had found a gold cup in the water 'with crosses on'. He had used the money to buy this filthy, dangerous hulk. How much treasure must be lying with the bones. So many must have gone down trying to escape to the last refuge. 'Aghtamar', the desperate cry of the drowning lover, 'Agh Tamar'.

As we stepped ashore, the soldiers shouted to us to be back at the landing punctually at sunset. I was too excited to mind anything, only thankful to have arrived. It was hard to believe I had actually arrived in front of Aghtamar, the apple of all Armenian eyes. The little church is one of the very few, almost the only, to be carved on the outside like an ivory casket. On the burnt-orange walls are allegorical stories: Jonah and the whale, Adam and Eve, portraits of Jesus and saints, all done with the happy confidence of a child bravely drawing Mummy and Daddy at his first school. The mixture of figures and animals, vines and flowers, is reminiscent of ancient Assyrian decoration but of a style entirely Armenian in originality. Happily, some of the frescoes inside the church have been allowed to remain, though the usual pigeon droppings are on the floor and altar. There were no candles to light, no signs even of cocks, of sheep having been sacrificed as one sometimes finds in apparently deserted churches in Soviet Armenia. No trees with prayer rags hopefully tied to the branches. No sign of care. We wandered out onto the rocky hillside in the wonderful sunshine; some of the party bathed off the black volcanic beaches. I climbed to the highest point on the tiny island where

King Gagic is supposed to have built a magnificent palace. I peered down gullies full of broken gravestones, all that Celtic tracery of interlaced patterns, so carefully carved, so proudly erected, broken up violently and now gently growing lichen. I walked in the shade of almond trees which could have been planted by Armenian monks on the garden terraces which were still visible. The ground was strewn with nuts, still in their green flannel jackets. The soldiers were cracking them on stones and eating them. Heaps of shells lay round about. There was nothing much else for them to do all day. We were herded back on board the reeking boat and got back to shore without disaster. As we walked away, my companion took something out of her pocket and opened her palm: five almonds. 'One for each of your children', she said.

Epilogue

When I got back, having lost half a stone in weight and feeling very old indeed from all the ancient places I had been to, I attended a series of lectures on Anatolian archaeology, given by a Turk. I sat near the front row wrapped in my Erzurum shawl. A large map was on the wall showing where I had just travelled – a very 'loud' map, the mountains bright orange, the plains bright green, the rivers thick and black, the highest mountains black caterpillars, writhing along from east to west, with Ararat erupting like a huge verruca. Had I really journeyed all that way? The lecturer's pointer travelled easily enough: 'Here is Ararat, here Lake Van'. The Armenians? Hardly a mention of them, the pointer sliding lightly on ('a lot to cover'), passing over so lightly the deserts in which my ancestors had died.

I travelled to Commagene, called Nimrud Dagh these days, not so very far from Maras and Urfa, but unknown to my nurse Makrouhi. Only shepherds and very energetic travellers went there before 1960 when the road was built. King Antiochus I, who thought he was god, lived the span of his life on earth about fifty years before Christ was born. He chose for his tomb one of the highest peaks of the Taurus and built on the top a pyramid another fifty feet high. The day we toiled up the splendid new road, handmade of cubes of black basalt patiently arranged in patterns by Turkish prisoners, was misty. At first, we felt rather than saw those unbelievable heads toppled this way and that, like so many sphinxes but so much more human.

These were Greek heads expressing human emotions: the colossal lips smiling, the vast eyes softened. Many miles away on the other side of the blue distance, they could have seen tombs of the women – mothers, wives, daughters, under another pyramid. As the mist cleared, we saw a stele: King Antiochus, dignified in tall cap and long robes, towering over Hercules, stark naked.

Driving all day in the rattling bus across dusty tablelands, our minds switched dizzily back and forth, from age to age: Antiochus, centuries after the Urartians, the Hittites, the Assyrians, but too early for even the first breath of Christianity. From Mardin, hanging like a gold honeycomb on the side of a mountain, we could see the whole of the Syrian and Mesopotamian plain, a grandstand view of a vast arena, stretching with scarcely an interruption, down to Saudi Arabia. Buildings of all ages were strewn across it, like children's toys on the floor, kicked about by earthquakes and invasions. We thundered across a 2,000-year-old Roman bridge; the next bridge is Seljuk, hundreds of years later, and neither of them repaired nor crumbling. We saw an ancient Armenian church, obstinately intact, though neglected, plants growing out of the cracks like hairs in an old man's nose, next to an equally venerable mosque. Anatolia is like a school blackboard, large enough for the next teacher to chalk in the next lesson without rubbing out the last. But on the old mosque's floor the deep litter of *kilims*, first begun when the mosque was new, thickening through hundreds of years, layer upon layer, is now being replaced by wall-to-wall carpeting, the old ones thrown out. So now priceless tatters hang on Hampstead walls, some of them hardly more than a few strands of wool held together by luck, the more ghostly, the more valuable. Though piled carpets were priceless as gold, *kilims* were not valued by my grandfather – they were for the servants' rooms, left out on the terrace through dust and rain storms. Each *kilim*, produced among the jumble of daily life, in a bedouin tent, is a memorial to the woman who wove it, her gift to the nearest mosque also, her masterpiece, her only claim to immortality. We passed 'gypsies' round their tents which were hardly more than wisps of rag huddled against the ruined wall of an old building – sometimes

Reverberations

a Seljuk caravanserai. I thought of their ancestors weaving rugs, dreaming their history into the patterns handed down from mother to daughter; in the figures, faint echoes of lost lands they would never see – Parthia perhaps or Scythia or Phrygia ... And in the markets I found rough wool socks. Some had crosses embroidered by Armenians, others bore the footprint of past invaders, Greek, Persian and Egyptian.

And as I gained weight after all my travels, I began to feel my lifelong nightmare lifting slowly from my mind like the low black cloud that often covers the top of the Old Man of Coniston in August.

As I was finishing this book, the devastating earthquake shattered part of the land I had travelled and reminded me that the country straddles two tectonic plates in constant motion, pulling apart and smashing together. Perhaps here was a clue to my father's character: he was always well aware of the clashing of his two worlds. Did his poetic self sometimes feel the pull of currents, deep down, sometimes causing unbearable tensions, sometimes colliding – occasionally causing earthquakes?

Five years later, in my Armenian friend's garden, there was blossom on the little tree grown from an almond picked up at Aghtamar.